Hoop Tales:
Maryland Terrapins
Men's Basketball

Hoop Tales® Series

Hoop Tales:
Maryland Terrapins Men's Basketball

Johnny Holliday
with
Stephen Moore

INSIDERS' GUIDE®

GUILFORD, CONNECTICUT
AN IMPRINT OF THE GLOBE PEQUOT PRESS

INSIDERS'GUIDE®

Text design: Casey Shain

All photos courtesy of Special Collections, University of Maryland Libraries, unless otherwise noted.

Cover photos: *front cover:* Juan Dixon (UM Department of Athletics); *back cover:* top, Len Bias shooting over Michael Jordan; bottom, Testudo with fans

Library of Congress Cataloging-in-Publication Data is available.

ISBN-13: 978-0-7627-3990-5
ISBN-10: 0-7627-3990-8

Manufactured in the United States of America
First Edition/First Printing

To all University of Maryland Terrapin fans
—Johnny Holliday

To Margaret, Charlie, and Suzy, with love
—Stephen Moore

Contents

Hatching the Turtle 1

True Believers 9

The Men in Striped Shirts 19

Duke Duels 31

Adrian Branch in OT 43

Lenny Bias 51

Billy, Walt, and Keith 63

Greatness by the Numbers 77

The Greatest Game Ever 97

Gary's Turning Points 105

Two Great Coaches 117

Champions 131

Home Court Advantages 147

Foreword

On the night of February 7, 2006, Gary Williams became the all-time winningest coach in Maryland basketball history, surpassing the legendary Lefty Driesell with his 349th victory at the school.

Not long after the game, Johnny Holliday walked into the Maryland locker room to tape Williams's weekly TV show with him. He offered Williams congratulations on the record. Williams, who rarely smiles on game day—before or after the game—smiled. "You've seen every one of these haven't you?" he said to Holliday. "I'm really glad you were a part of this—all of this."

I have no doubt that those words meant a lot to Johnny because, like me, he has known Gary Williams for a long time. He has not only seen all of Gary's wins at Maryland, but he also saw quite a few of Lefty's wins, calling play-by-play during the last seven years of Driesell's tenure in College Park. Heck, he even saw all of Bob Wade's wins.

All of which means there is no one more qualified to be your tour guide through any kind of history of Maryland basketball, whether it focuses on last season or twenty-five seasons ago, than Johnny Holliday. Not only has he been there all those years, but he really does know all the people who have been a part of the ups and the downs the program has gone through—not just the coaches but the players, the doctors, trainers, and even the reporters who have covered the team.

One of the things I have always admired about Johnny as a play-by-play man is that he approaches each game from the point of view of someone who has played a lot of basketball. Johnny may have played in more charity basketball games than anyone who has ever lived, and he played not just as some celebrity out there having fun or entertaining, but as a PLAYER. (His teammates will tell you that Johnny never shot unless he actually had the ball in his hands.) Because he has the mentality of a player, Johnny understands the rhythms of the game and what it feels like to win a big game or to lose a big game. I think one of the reasons Gary has enjoyed working with Johnny all these years—and the list of people Gary enjoys working with isn't a very long one—is that Johnny never asks a dumb question. He asks the kinds of questions a player or coach would think to ask before or after a game.

I had the good fortune to be assigned the Maryland beat at the *Washington Post* the same year (1979, when I was twelve) that Johnny took over the play-by-play. I learned a lot by watching the way Johnny interacted with the people around the program. He had—and has—the almost unique ability to clearly be part of the program and the team without being a shill. Everyone who listens to Johnny knows he wants Maryland to win. But you will never hear him say "we" on the air, and when someone on the other team makes a play, Johnny gives credit where credit is due—unlike his partner Chris Knoche, who tends to blame everything on the officials. Of course, that's what ex-coaches do.

I have no doubt you will enjoy this trip down memory lane with Johnny. As Gary Williams points out, Johnny has seen a lot of Maryland basketball through the years. In fact, I think the case can be made that there's no one alive who has seen more Maryland basketball the last twenty-seven years or knows more about Maryland basketball than Johnny. And think what those twenty-seven years have been like: the great Lefty-versus-Dean Smith battles, Lefty's historic win at the ACC Tournament in 1984, the triumph and tragedy of Len Bias, Gary's revival of the program, and, of course, the national championship in 2002 in Atlanta.

I remember the night of the championship vividly. At almost the same time that Johnny was taking over as the voice of Maryland basketball, a young coach named Gary Williams was getting his first coaching job at American University. Gary and I became friends back then in large part because we were both basketball junkies. On nights when Maryland wasn't playing, I would sneak over to Ft. Myer in Virginia to watch Gary's teams play. I knew I was watching a rising star in the coaching business. On the night Maryland won the national title, I was on the court after the game and congratulated Gary. He put his arm around me and said, "We're a long way from Ft. Myer, aren't we?" Then he said, "I gotta go do my postgame with Johnny."

Which, of course, he did. Because Johnny was there that night too. Just as he has been right there for so many nights that Maryland has played basketball.

—John Feinstein

Acknowledgments

We appreciate this opportunity to celebrate the 150th anniversary of the University of Maryland by sharing selected stories of the renowned men's basketball program. Our thanks to Patrick Straub at Globe Pequot for inviting us to this project and for providing superb editorial guidance throughout the process.

Many fine folks contributed to this volume. We thank coaches Gary Williams, Bud Millikan, and Lefty Driesell for sharing experiences, thoughts, and feelings. We enormously appreciate John Feinstein's foreword. John is a good friend.

We immensely value the time and efforts of university archivist Ann Turkos at Hornbake Library. Despite her rigorous schedule of preparing a multitude of production projects for UM anniversary celebrations, Ann was always ready and willing to help us with research and many of the photos that went into *Hoop Tales.* The only time she was unavailable was when the women's basketball team took the court. There's no question that Ann is one of the hardest-working people on campus.

With sincere gratitude we thank the many players, officials, and fans who contributed comments to our cause, including Jeff Baxter, Steve Bisciotti, Steve Blake, Adrian Branch, Doug Dull, Duke Edsall, Governor Robert Ehrlich, Jason Frankel, Barry Gossett, Donnie Gray, Tony Green, Mike Grinnon, Jack Heise, Tahj Holden, Jim Johnson, Billy Jones, Albert King, Keith Neff, Robert Novak, Marv Perry, Dr. Irv Raffle, Stand Rote, Duane Simpkins, Buck Williams, Walt Williams, Lennie Wirtz, and Jack Zane.

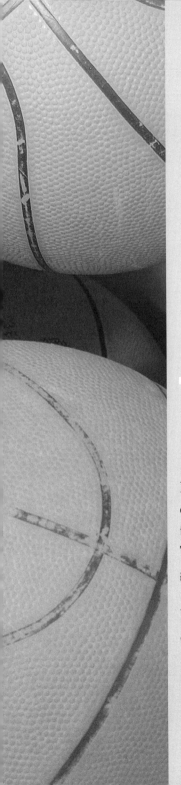

Hatching the Turtle

Everyone who understands basketball knows of its origin. In 1891 Dr. James Naismith, of the Springfield, Massachusetts, YMCA Training School, proposed an indoor winter game to keep physical education students interested in fitness. Two half-bushel peach baskets inspired the game's name. Basketball quickly caught on at many colleges, and Naismith lived to see his invention included in the 1936 Olympics.

One year after Naismith created the game, Maurice Joyce (1851–1939), a former circus trapeze artist and United States marshal, introduced basketball to the Washington, D.C., area. Joyce came to the city to direct a local athletic club known as the Carroll Institute. The *Evening Star* reported that Joyce hung chairs upside down as goals when peach baskets weren't available. (Today the coaches are hung upside down when they don't have winning seasons.) Some believe that Joyce's structured five-man squad in the District was the first in the nation. So far we've found nobody to dispute that claim.

In 1895 the *Washington Post* ran the following news item: "A meeting of the athletes of Carroll Institute will be held in the gymnasium tomorrow night for the purpose of forming a basketball league . . . Prof. Joyce is an enthusiast on the subject and believes there are enough devotees to form a successful league."

Professor Joyce was a man with real flair, and he made sure basketball was in Washington to stay. Meanwhile, 10 miles up Route 1, sports got a slow start at humble Maryland Agricultural College (MAC). Maryland's first informal basketball squad, captained by Samuel P. Thomas, didn't appear until 1905. "During the winter months with simply a football game now and then, life became very monotonous," reported the school yearbook, the *Reveille*. "Until some ingenious mind conceived of the idea of basketball."

The MAC squad—known as the "Aggies," or just as often, "the Farmers"—lost its first two games to YMCA and Carroll Institute squads. Not a good beginning, but a year later the bottoms of the baskets were removed so players didn't have to retrieve the ball after each successful shot. This minor adjustment proved to be a major boon in increasing the excitement of

Fear the early Turtles.

the game—and a few wins would increase it even more.

By 1911 the Aggies started to get some traction. H. Burton (Burt) Shipley, an aggressive and well-liked football player, was named team captain. Burt freely admitted that he couldn't shoot, but as a back guard he held his own defensively and would often distract his opponents by slamming his foot on the court. Burt could have easily played for Lefty Driesell, who broke his own foot after doing the "Lefty stomp" during a heated game many years later.

Home games were held in a crowded Sunday school gym in nearby Berwyn Heights. The Aggies' game plan included running opponents into the radiators located in the walls of the gym, especially if the opponent had a player with a hot hand. Still, the 1910–11 team record was a dismal 3–9.

That gym had to serve until interest in the program gained some momentum, especially since most everything on campus except Morris Hall had been destroyed a year earlier in a fire that broke out during a Thanksgiving dance. With no campus gym, the Aggies practiced only three times that season. Nobody expected wonders from Burt's basketball team; just keeping basketball going on campus was the overriding goal.

One of the first contests to create some positive notoriety for the Aggies—and to be reported in the *Washington Post*—came against Baltimore City College two seasons later. City College's squad was light and speedy, scoring on four shots and a foul in the first minutes of the game. The Aggies came alive later in the first half to use their superior weight to their advantage. But at the break, Maryland still trailed 16–14.

The Aggies jumped out to a 3-point lead early in the second half. They increased that lead to 5 points before City College rallied to send the game into overtime. City College scored the first 3 points in OT before William "Country" Morris and C. F. Huntmann hit back-to-back field goals to put Maryland up by 1, for a final score of 30–29. Shipley, Kenneth Cole, Morris, Huntmann, and Stanley Day played the entire game, while City College had but one substitution. On the defensive end Day was outstanding.

Shipley, class of 1914, would go on to earn eleven athletic letters at Maryland. He returned to coach basketball for twenty-

H. Burton Shipley in his football togs.

four seasons and baseball for thirty-seven and was in the first group of inductees of the University of Maryland Athletic Hall of Fame. His basketball record is 243–199, with a Southern Conference record of 124–91. "Do Something, Ship" became the ubiquitous student cheer at games he coached.

The return of Harry C. "Curly" Byrd (class of 1908) to campus in the autumn of 1911 as assistant manager of athletics and general coach proved extremely important in its effect on the future of sports at College Park. A native of Crisfield, Maryland, Byrd had been a stellar, multitalented student athlete: He served as captain of the football team and as a pitcher on the baseball team, and he set the school record of 10.0 seconds in the 100-yard dash. It is claimed that Byrd was the first quarterback in the East to master the forward pass, five years before Notre Dame's Gus Dorais in 1914.

Byrd never played basketball, but he had a progressive outlook on sports and was an inspirational coaching success. Over fifteen years he led the football, baseball, basketball, track, and tennis teams to conference championships and the cross-country and lacrosse teams to national championships.

"Curly had a photographic mind, and it served him well," Shipley recalled in Kent Baker's excellent basketball history *Red, White, and Amen*. "One time," recalled Buddy Emmons, another early Maryland basketball player, "I split an ear open during a game. Curley had the answer. He went and got a football helmet, put it on me, and sent me back in."

MAC was renamed Maryland State College in 1916, and for one season (1918–19) the Aggies played in the District Intercollegiate Basketball League against Gallaudet, Catholic, and George Washington Universities. All games were held in the old

Washington, D.C., YMCA. After a five-game losing streak at the conclusion of the 1919 season, Maryland basketball disappeared.

In 1920 Maryland State merged with the professional schools in Baltimore to become the University of Maryland, and the basketball program resumed in 1923 under Shipley and Byrd in its new campus facility, the Gymnasium, inside Annapolis Hall. After an opening season record of 5–7, Maryland's first officially recognized varsity team improved to a 14–3 record three seasons later and to 16–4 by 1932.

In 1933 Byrd, who was on his way to becoming university president, suggested the terrapin as the team's mascot. The newly christened Maryland Terrapins basketball team was now a reputable and determined contender, ready to build a competitive heritage.

Driving to the Hoop

In *Red, White, and Amen,* author Kent Baker describes the style of early twentieth-century basketball like so: "Basketball in the 1920s reflected the carefree style of the period. It was characterized by a rough-and-tumble style of play with an abundance of fouling." Baker credits Jack Faber, a member of Maryland's early team, with this observation: "The man with the ball had the privilege of driving to the basket. If anybody got in his way, it was too bad."

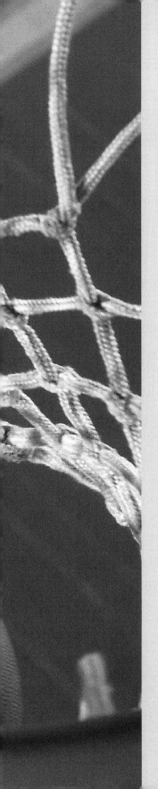

True Believers

Ask any coach in America and he or she will tell you without question that fans, especially at home games, are in essence the "sixth man" who helps propel the team to victory. This is evident at the University of Maryland, where Terp fans have taken it to the next level with their enthusiasm, knowledge, and passionate, unwavering support of the program.

Fans know that Maryland owns Midnight Madness. Coach Lefty Driesell came up with the idea when he proposed to start practice at the earliest moment allowed under NCAA rules. The tradition was born on October 15, 1970, in Cole Field House.

Today, the event is the definitive pep rally for all college teams, but nobody does it better than Maryland. Spectators are likely to see such notable fans as Governor Robert Ehrlich Jr. with his young son, Drew; Baltimore Ravens owner Steve Bisciotti; *Face the Nation* moderator Tim Russert; syndicated columnist and TV moderator Robert Novak; Montgomery County executive Doug Duncan; and faithful former Terps like Walt Williams, Jim O'Brien, Jeff Baxter, Ernie Graham, and many others who, despite their wild schedules, still find time to come back home to root for their alma mater.

Carol Harris—an alum, attorney, and amateur golfer—says, "I was at the 1966 championship game at Cole Field House [Texas Western vs. Kentucky]. I love Maryland. The program is something to be proud of, and watching Maryland basketball is transporting. You can forget everything else, and that's why I come."

Keith Neff, one of Coach Williams's closest supporters, never misses a game. "No question about it," says Neff. "I went to school here in the early '70s and got hooked on Terps basketball. It is a family. I'm very proud of our state school. It's been a dream come true winning a NCAA national championship, an ACC Tournament title, and two Final Fours. I'll take our fans any day. It just doesn't get any better."

Superfan Profile

Name: Steve Bisciotti

Hometown: Severna Park, Maryland

Occupation: Owner, Baltimore Ravens

First Terps game: 1975, in Cole Field House

First season tickets: 1993—"It was good timing courtside, as Joe Smith and Keith Booth were freshmen, Duane Simpkins and Exree Hipp were sophomores, Gary Williams began winning, and I thought Walt Williams was a god for staying with him."

Courtside advantages: "The refs don't take my comments very seriously. I think I've probably only influenced two calls in ten years. I think I should get a better return on my investment."

On similarities between the Terps and the Ravens: "We won our Super Bowl in 2001, and Gary made the Final Four two months later. Gary teased me by complaining that he'd been trying for a championship for twenty-seven years, and I bought a team and won the Super Bowl in the first year."

On Gary Williams: "Because we're friends, I get a chance to see Gary on and off the court. Gary and his passion about what he does, how he cares about his players, and how much he loves his job fascinate me."

Gary Williams on Steve: "What really strikes me about Steve Bisciotti is his loyalty to the friends he's had forever. A lot of people, when they become very successful like Steve, move on. His friends are the same ones he grew up with. That's one of his strengths."

Robert Novak

One of the most faithful Terps supporters is Robert Novak, a conservative syndicated columnist for the *Chicago Sun-Times* and a television commentator with CNN and Fox News. He works his schedule around the team, travels on the team plane, and rarely misses a game. People say he's a little crazy about the Terps, and he agrees "that's a given." Novak says that wins on the road are especially "delicious," while the trips back on the team plane after a loss are like "a death in the family."

Novak's first Terps experience came when he took his father, a big basketball fan, to a Maryland-Duke game at Cole Field House in 1969. "It was Lefty's first season," Novak recalls. "Duke was ranked twelfth in the country; Maryland didn't have much of a team then. The *Washington Post* said that the 12,000 fans there was an 'unusually large crowd.' Maryland won in the last seconds by a long shot from the middle of the floor by Will Hetzel. It was a terrific upset, and I got hooked."

As a season ticket-holder since 1971 and a member of the Terrapins Club (composed of alumni, friends, and fans of Maryland athletics), Novak has seen the fans change over the years. "Cole was not known as a demonstrative place when I started going," he recalls, and "fans didn't use to wear red. People always talk about things getting worse, but sometimes they get better. For example, the African-American fans used to sit together, and there was enormous racial tensions in those days, so things have really improved there."

Novak used to say that if the Terps could only get to the Final Four, then he would be happy. "But we went to the Final Four and I wasn't happy *because we didn't win*," he recalls now. "But we returned and won the championship. I do think we had the best team in the country then. We only lost four games that year, and Connecticut had the second-best team. We beat them twice."

About Gary Williams, Novak says, "I'm very fond of Gary. He's enormously popular, and I suppose some criticize him, but that comes with the territory of being in the public eye. . . . The real fans love Gary for what he's brought to the program."

Of all the Terps players, Novak ranks Len Bias and Juan Dixon at the top. "Len was the greatest collegiate player, and Juan was just all heart and could will the team to win. Len was a hard player and a soft player. Very tough inside, very muscular, but silky soft on his jump shot. He could do it all."

The Courtmaster

Jim Johnson, aka "The Courtmaster" (www.thecourtmaster.net), has been a huge Terps fan since watching Maryland's 31–30 victory over number two South Carolina in 1971 on his black-and-white TV. His passion for Maryland has intensified over the years, especially after he earned a degree from University College.

This passion has not always proved positive. "I remember leaving Cole Field House after watching Maryland fritter away a game against number one North Carolina in 1984," Johnson recalls. "My best friend, Robin, trudged with me through 20-degree weather, and we took turns ranting, 'Why do we do this to ourselves?' " But because of their passion for the Terps, the two would repeat that exercise many times over the years.

"My late wife, Bette . . . never did get over seeing me on all fours, pounding the floor during an ACC Tournament game in 1999 that the Terps lost to North Carolina. It took all summer to convince her to watch another game with me. Bette knew that she could tweak me when talking about Maryland hoops by saying, 'Don't worry, it's only a game,' but I was never able to explain the utter absurdity of that statement," Johnson says.

On the Terps championship night of April 1, 2002, Bette learned just how deep her husband's love for the team ran. As the clock wound down and the game was in hand, he laid his head on her shoulder and cried like a baby. Thirty-two years of tragedy and painful losses poured out through his tears.

"When I looked up, Bette's moist eyes met mine with a look of realization," Johnson recalls. "She got it! Bette now understood why I had invested so much of myself in Terps basketball—holding onto the hope of the moment when my school would become a champion.

"Now that Bette is in heaven, I hold that night among my most treasured memories. I look forward to my [new] wife Brenda and me making our own Maryland memories . . . The Terps won the first two Duke games Brenda and I watched together, a promising beginning."

Testudo

One ubiquitous part of any Terps game is Testudo, the costumed mascot. The identity of the student inside the Testudo suit appears to be a Maryland secret. We asked university officials to arrange an interview with the current Testudo. The answer was "no interviews with the mascot." Nonetheless, those who have sweated, pranced, and danced their way through thousands of basketball games over the years deserve some recognition and sincere thanks.

Former student Andrea Koeppel was chosen in the school's first Testudo audition, in 1978. The university did not fund an official suit at the time, so she appeared in a homemade costume. Koeppel said that she looked more like a green lizard than a turtle, couldn't see well, and was, as might be expected, *very hot.*

But she loved it.

Jason Frankel started out as a golden retriever for University of Maryland, Baltimore County, before he transferred to UM in 2000. "I went from being a big dog to a big turtle," he says. According to Frankel, he abided by the three primo rules of being Testudo: 1. You can't talk. 2. You can't be seen in a partial costume. ("This is especially important because small children really believe you *are* a big turtle.") 3. You represent the university, so no obscene gestures, like flicking the middle finger, or getting into fights.

Frankel, who graduated with a degree in computer science, likens his four-year stint as Testudo to "being somewhat like a superhero. You couldn't reveal your identity, although [it was] hard to keep that secret from my girlfriend when she saw the giant costume in my dorm room."

The highlight of Frankel's mascot career came in 2001: "The Terps were playing the number one seed, the Stanford Cardinal, going to our first Final Four. Lonny Baxter won the regional MVP award. I remember this distinctly, because the Stanford

Testudo the Terrapin

Here are some fun facts about Maryland's beloved mascot:

- The terrapin is a 300-million-year-old aquatic reptile of the order *Testudines* (the Latin term for a movable protective covering used by Roman soldiers).

- Testudo was named the mascot in 1933 by coach and future university president Harry "Curly" Byrd, a Crisfield, Maryland, native fond of the local diamondback terrapins.

- The first living Testudo, 5 inches tall with a green shell, is now preserved at the Hornebake Library and is protected by university archivist Ann Turkos.

- A 300-pound bronze sculpture of Testudo originally was mounted in front of Ritchie Coliseum, a gift from the class of 1933. In 1965 Testudo took his final position in front of McKeldin Library, reinforced by concrete and steel.

- In the 1980s the mascot began to appear at games.

- In 2001 fans began chanting "Fear the Turtle" during the team's trip to the NCAA Final Four.

- In 2004 Testudo was named to the Capital One All-America Mascot Team, an honor granted to only twelve university mascots in the country.

Testudo and fans have better things to do than watch the opposing players being introduced.
UM Athletic Department

players were crying after Maryland won, and I was crying tears of joy. Terrance Morris jumped up into the stands and hugged his mom. Juan Dixon was going crazy. The emotion was extraordinary. When they were ready to cut the net, I was at the foot of the ladder. Juan handed me the game ball to hold while he climbed up. I'll carry that memory until the day I die."

Frankel is certainly not alone. School supporter Barry Gossett (the Gossett team house, a $7 million home for Terps football, is named after him) can always be seen cheering courtside under the basket. He says, "I've been involved since I was ten years old as an usher at Byrd Stadium. You get a quality education here, and you always could, although some people didn't know that in the past. Terps games are a natural for me because I get to meet so many good people, and it is just fun."

Another Terps benefactor, Dr. Irv Raffle, echoes Gossett's pride in Maryland academics and sports: "Maryland is a great institution. I believe heavily in the public school environment. I enjoy helping the school where I got an education and a degree to enable me to be successful in life. I'm just giving back some of what was given to me, and I love it, too. The environment here at Comcast [Center] is second to none. It's great to be at these games, and everyone should try to make it a part of their life."

Go Terps.

The Men in Striped Shirts

Fans do not come to games to see men in striped shirts blowing whistles. They come to see the players play. When you don't notice the officials during a game, then they've done a good job. When they constantly have confrontations with players or coaches, especially "disagreements" that get the fans all riled up, then it may not be one of their better nights.

Veteran referee Lenny Wirtz, who retired in 1995 after forty years of officiating, doesn't agree. The colorful and often outspoken Wirtz says that his advice for young officials after the buzzer sounds is this: "If 50 percent of the people love you, then you've done a good job. But if you walk off and 100 percent hate you, then you've done an *outstanding* job."

Wirtz says that when he began officiating in 1955, Cole Field House and Reynolds Coliseum were the best facilities on the East Coast. He officiated two Final Fours at Cole and decided early on that he wouldn't take a lot of flack from coaches. "If they started giving me a lot of grief, then I might tell the coach, 'Look, you made your call for the night, and you missed it.' But I wouldn't listen to them referee. If they didn't settle down, I would just bang 'em with a technical foul and get it over with."

Official Duties

"Sports officials must be able to bring control to chaos; understand fairness; promote safety and encourage good sportsmanship. A sports official must have the positive characteristics of a police officer, lawyer, judge, accountant, reporter, athlete and diplomat."

—The National Association of Sports Officials

Wirtz has great respect for all three Maryland coaches he worked with, beginning with Bud Millikan. "Bud was a true gentleman and one of the greatest coaches I ever refereed for," he says. "I was there when Gary Williams played for Bud, and the coach was one of these guys who was so nice."

But Millikan had a habit of gently protesting calls. "You know, when I see the films . . ." he would say, suggesting that the films would prove him right. "He pulled that twice with me one night," Wirtz recalls, "and then there was an out-of-bounds play right at his bench in the Terps' favor. I blew the whistle and then sat down next to his team. Bud yelled, 'What are you doing?' I responded, 'I'm going to wait for the films.'"

Point made.

For memories of Lefty Driesell, Wirtz goes back to the coach's days at Davidson before he came to UM. "In those days Lefty was driving an old Chevrolet, [and] he used a rag to hold the door shut. When he was getting started, he didn't have a budget to recruit, so he'd sleep in his car when he was making the recruitment rounds.

"Lefty became such a showman," Wirtz says. "At Maryland he'd come on the floor with 'Hail to the Chief' blaring through the Cole speakers." Wirtz once reminded him, "You might be the chief walking on, but you're going to have to earn it when you walk off."

Terp fans know that Driesell became famous for stomping his foot to punctuate his emotions. "When he'd start acting up and stomping that damn foot, then I'd go over next to him and start stomping my own foot," laughs Wirtz. "I'd tell him, 'The next time your foot's going to be underneath mine.'"

In reference to Gary Williams, Wirtz says that the coach has always been very excitable. "Even back when he came from Ohio State, he was getting all worked up and sweating profusely. Once during a close game I asked him, 'What the hell are you getting so excited about? I'm the one catching all the hell out here.' " Williams yelled back, "I'm trying to win."

"Gary is hard-nosed, and if you push him, then he'll take the technical foul just to show you he won't be challenged. But if you handle him with respect, then it works out well."

* * *

The frustrated coach protesting an official's call is often as essential to a great Terps game as the slam dunk and the three-point shot. These days at the Comcast Center, you will find all eyes on Williams when the back-and-forth with officials begins. "Gary Williams brings intensity," says Donnie Gray, who's been refereeing games since 1985 and has four Final Fours and an NCAA championship game under his belt. "Gary is a super coach. But when I'm refereeing a game, Gary Williams is no different to me than any other coach. He knows that, as do all the other coaches in the games I referee."

In Gray's mind, the most important thing an official needs to understand is subtle differences between a coach's opinion and his attitude, as well as recognize when he or she is just seeking information. Donnie explains: "Gary Williams could be seeking information even while he's yelling with his arms in the air. People can get the impression that he's on me, but maybe he's telling me that the clock's not running or that one of his players is hurt."

When an attitude develops, the coach might cross the line. That's why Gray never ignores a coach: In most cases, if you give

Maryland Victory Song

Maryland, we're all behind you.
Wave high the BLACK and GOLD,
For there is nothing half so glorious
As to see our team victorious.
We've got the team, Terps,
We've got the steam, Terps,
So keep on fighting, don't give in!
M-A-R-Y-L-A-N-D
Maryland will win!

that coach an ear and act professionally, you can clear up an argumentative situation in a few seconds. You can't spend time giving the coach a clinic, but you must give a reasonable answer.

"Gary is like some of the toughest coaches in the country—like John Thompson, Dean Smith," Gray says. "And like other tough coaches from my personal experience: They turn out to be the easiest ones to work for. They expect their players to work hard just as they work hard, and they want the officials to work just as hard."

Gray remembers one night when Williams wanted a goal-tending call. Gray refused, but the coach wasn't buying it.

"How about you tell me the three parts of goal tending," Gray demanded. Williams shot back, "I don't know."

"Well, I guess you'll just have to trust me." Gray smiled.

After the game, Gray showered and came out of the locker room, and there was Williams standing next to the door with a rule book. "He let me know that I was right. And we both laughed."

When Gray isn't officiating Terps games, he's the validation clerk for the U.S. Senate, making sure that what goes in the permanent Senate record is correct. But on game day, it is Gray who gets the final word. "Many people helped me out when I first started officiating Boy's Clubs and CYO games in 1976," he says, "especially Tommy Scott, Jimmy Howell, and Pete Barnett. They taught me to have an ear for everybody, to not only listen to successful refs, but also to listen to those who made mistakes."

Gray says that as much as the games at different schools are alike, they also differ. The focus can be on fairness or on jeering the opposite team and calling into question every ruling that goes against the home team. "Maryland has a winning tradition, and this was true even when UM wasn't having successful years," says Gray. "When Walt Williams was at Cole, for example, you could feel the excitement and tension at Maryland."

Gray recalls his early games with Driesell: "Lefty was a very nice man. He'd ask me a question maybe once every five or ten minutes but really never bothered the officials. He concentrated on coaching his team. He was no different at Maryland than when I worked his games at James Madison, although those programs were hugely different."

Today, Gray thinks that the fans—especially the highly connected financial contributors sitting courtside—feel that they're close to the officials and can question calls more aggressively. "One night, a guy was going ballistic on me. Eyes bulging, veins popping in his neck," recalls Gray, who replied, "Sir, I'd just like to compliment you on your dress and your lovely wife and how handsome you both look."

The fan shot back at Gray about his officiating, and Gray finally said, "Listen, we're getting the calls right." But the fan kept talking. Finally, Gray said, "Look, the way you are acting, you're going to have a heart attack or a stroke. I'm a paramedic, and if that happens, I'm going to let you die."

Everyone started laughing, and the guy quieted down. But then Gray looked over and the fan was just sitting there, not cheering or smiling. So a few minutes later, Gray offered to teach the fan a little about the game if he had some time later.

This ref psychology obviously worked, because at the next game when the fan saw Gray, he jumped up, pointed, and yelled, "That's my man! That's my man!"

* * *

Another face familiar to longtime Terps fans is Stan Rote, who began officiating CYO ball in West Virginia when he was ten years old. Stan retired at age fifty-nine in 1999 because, in his words, "A sixty-year-old referee is repulsive to me, and the younger refs all cheered, because they wanted my games."

After Rote's retirement, he returned as an official observer at UM. He got into a controversy, however, when he objected to fans who cursed the opponents, especially in conjunction with songs by the school band. The school newspaper wrote him up, but Rote still did not feel that these derogatory cheers were appropriate, and Coach Williams agreed with him. "Gary picked up the microphone and reminded the fans that they're better than that," Rote recalls. "Things were handled after that."

Rote says that Duke-versus-Maryland contests, because of the excitement and the pressure, became "the most difficult games to work for all the referees, especially in Duke's Cameron Indoor Stadium, where the fans are right on top of you."

Rote's call against a Maryland shot at the buzzer gave Duke a win in 1996. "I thought the time ran out, but everyone in the world thought I screwed up the call, especially after all the network sports shows were replaying that shot and saying it was wrong. I said then that if I was wrong, I'd quit the league." (If you look at the video, you'll see that the Maryland player took the shot and that it was 6 feet from his hand when the clock ran out.)

Spectators may not appreciate that the referee has a unique perspective on the game. You almost have to be in his shoes and see plays from his exact line of sight to properly challenge what the referee thinks happened.

"One thing about Maryland that people may not understand," Rote says, "is that if you check the records regarding technical fouls against players in the ACC over the last twenty-five years, you'll find that Maryland has very, very few technical fouls. The Maryland kids have always been the easy ones to referee. The Terps play the game hard and fair."

Rote points to former North Carolina Tar Heel Rasheed Wallace as the best example of the opposite. "Rasheed would come down the court late after a rebound and hold his elbow high to bump players in the face so it would look inadvertent. You had to babysit the guy because all these dumb things would happen when he was playing. Maryland players were never like this."

Rote has known Gary Williams for thirty years, going back to Williams's days at American University, and states flat out that no coach works harder. "Gary's a different guy when the game is over, but once the ball goes up, it is strictly work." Rote attests. "His intensity is incredible. Early on, when he first came to Maryland, there was a perception in the league that other schools would 'get the close calls.' I think Gary felt that, too, thinking that Maryland hadn't earned the status of some of the other schools. Gary knew he'd have to win."

Rote believes that Williams felt the pressure of carrying the entire Maryland athletic program, especially "when the football team wasn't doing anything either."

"Once Gary won the championship," Rote offers, "he began to accept things and let some of the minor things go. He's more mature, naturally, but he still coaches the same way. He listens to the refs, and he's still sweating through those suits."

* * *

The ref who may know Williams's coaching best is Duke Edsall, who began officiating ACC games in 1982. He holds the distinction of refereeing Williams's first game at Cole Field House, against Delaware State, and his final Cole game against Virginia. And many in between.

"The Delaware game was a unique situation," Edsall recalls. "Gary already had a reputation for being a little wild on the sidelines. We had a conversation that we don't do these kind of things in the ACC, but three minutes into the game, I had to give him a technical foul. I'm sure he remembers."

"Gary wears his emotions on his sleeve," Edsall continues. "But most of the time he's not even in our ear, although it may look that way to the fans. He's jumping up and down, but people don't always understand that he's not really as bad as he looks. Gary is actually one of the fairest coaches I've known."

The brother of UConn football coach Randy Edsall, Duke began his Maryland association as a kid growing up in York, Pennsylvania, when he attended Driesell's basketball camp. Refereeing the last game at Cole was the biggest thrill of his career, partly because he worked his first league game—Maryland versus Duke—at Cole.

From a twenty-five-year-plus perspective, Edsall believes that we see better athletes today, but not necessarily better basketball players: "In terms of skill levels and fundamentals of the game, I don't believe the players today are as good as those in the early '80s," he attests, "but collectively the teams now have better athletes. And it's tough to keep up with them. The guys are quicker, bigger, stronger, faster, and they're shooting from longer range."

Edsall quickly cites Len Bias as the greatest collegiate basketball player. "Absolutely. Len is the best player I've seen on the floor in my twenty-five years in the ACC. I've never seen a player better dominate the game. Len Bias put the team on his shoulders."

Like all officials, Edsall has to manage the players and coaches, and he does so by talking to them throughout the game. If he can gain their trust and talk them out of doing things he'll have to call, then it's a better game all around. "For example, if I know I have a player who has a tendency to palm the ball, then while we're walking up the court I'll tell him, 'Be careful on the palming today,' " Edsall says. "You develop a relationship with these kids over four years. I try to gain their trust."

Official Duke Edsall has been refereeing ACC games for a quarter of a century.
Courtesy of Duke Edsall

Edsall tells everybody this: If the players shoot 50 percent or better, then the refs are going to look great out there. If the refs have to make a million decisions, then it's not so good.

Duke Duels

Juan Dixon, Steve Blake, Tahj Holden, Byron Mouton, Lonny Baxter, and the rest of the 2001–02 team are among my favorites of all the Maryland teams I've covered. They were personable, funny, accommodating, accessible, and a great bunch of guys. They proved how great they were on February 17, 2002, in their upset victory over archrival Duke. Maryland led from start to finish, winning 87–73.

It was the final game between the Terps and the Blue Devils held at Cole Field House, and it was one of the most exciting games I ever called at Cole. Duke was the last undefeated team in the country. Chris Wilcox had 23 points for Maryland that day.

Fans will remember the steal by Blake, who was defending Jason Williams. Blake was better known for his assists—he led his team in assists all four years he played at UM—but his picking the pocket of Williams is one of the finest defensive plays I've witnessed. "That was the biggest individual play of my career," says Blake. "Jason turned his head, and I went after the ball with no thought. I was able to take the shot, and it was pretty exciting for me."

I once asked Blake about his personal approach against players of Williams's caliber. "To be the best, you've got to play the best," said Blake. "You have to know their tendencies, strengths, and weaknesses. You have to anticipate what they like to do in certain situations and remember how that player has played against you in past games. You have to watch the films, and then you have to go out and play 100 percent and see what happens."

The Duke rivalry went to the next level with Maryland's 2004 win in Greensboro for their first ACC Tournament title in twenty years. With a final score of 95–87, the overtime thriller snapped the top-seeded Blue Devils' run at five straight championships. Junior guard John Gilchrist, from Virginia Beach, Virginia, led the Terrapins with 26 points and was named tournament MVP. Gilchrist had scored 30 against NC State and 16 against Wake Forest to lead the Terps to the Duke showdown. Going back to 1904–05, only two other Maryland teams had won the ACC Tournament: one for Coach Bud Millikan (1957–58) and one for Lefty Driesell (1983–84).

The 2004 ACC championship game was a battle from start to finish. Maryland led by as many as 11 in the first half, but Duke forged ahead to go up by 12 with only 4:58 left in the game. Not to be denied, the Terps came right back on a 15–3 run to tie the game at 77 and force overtime. Maryland outscored Duke 18–10 in the extra five minutes to win it, cut down the nets, and bring the tournament trophy back to College Park.

In 2005, after Maryland's third straight win over Duke, the Blue Devils's J. J. Redick conceded that the Maryland-Duke rivalry is as intense as any college rivalry—perhaps more so than Carolina-Duke. "The Maryland-Duke rivalry is a little more about hate," Redick told *USA Today*. "Maryland is the most hostile environment we play in. Their students are right on top of you, and there's so many of them in that new Comcast arena. They're always loud, they're always yelling. And it's a really tough place to play."

Terp fans agree. The Duke duels are the most watched and anticipated games of the year. They draw the highest ratings on ESPN, and many are included in the network's "classics" file.

* * *

Though there wasn't much of a rivalry going on in the Driesell era—then, it was more NC State and North Carolina that commanded the attention of fans—there's no question that beating Duke since Gary Williams has arrived is very satisfying. "You don't gloat. You just feel good because you beat a great program and a great coach," says Williams.

The Driesell-era rivalry was first sharpened with the February 2, 1980, appearance of "Wild Bill" Haggy, better known for his spirited cheers at nearby Baltimore Orioles games. Wild Bill surprised the fans attending the sold-out Cole game against Duke, and instead of spelling out ORIOLES with his frenetic body language, he spelled out TERPS. The crowd went nuts. Even the players noticed. Albert King said, "Wild Bill coming from Baltimore to Cole to lead the cheers really got the players pumped up."

It worked. All five of Driesell's starters—Ernie Graham (12), Albert King (16), Buck Williams (18), Reggie Jackson (11), and Greg Manning (26)—finished in double figures.

Manning, an All-ACC selection for three straight years, was a standout guard who could run the floor with the best of them. (Later, in 1991, Maryland athletic director Andy Geiger hired Manning to be my color analyst on radio broadcasts. Our professional relationship lasted fourteen seasons. They don't come any finer than him.) Manning's performance was so dominating against Duke that it prompted Blue Devils head coach Bill Foster to call him "the most underrated player in the ACC."

Manning's teammate Buck Williams might have wanted to argue that point. Williams was going against the ACC's leading scorer and rebounder, Mike Gminski. Williams outscored Gminski 18–17 while collecting 12 rebounds and was named player of the game. The Terrapins improved to 16–3 overall and 8–1 in the ACC, taking a two-game lead over North Carolina for the top spot in the conference.

The Terps pushed their lead against the Blue Devils to 18 midway through the second half. But then they lost their focus, and Duke closed within 9 before Driesell stomped his foot and called a time-out.

The coach obviously got his team's attention: They returned to score 8 straight points to lead by 14. So dominant was Maryland's performance that with 2:13 remaining, Driesell had the

Maryland versus Duke in Overtime

Date	Home/Away	Win/Loss	Score
2/20/32	A	W	20–18
3/7/58	ACC*	W	71–65
1/14/67	ACC	L	69–72
3/4/76	ACC	W	80–78
2/5/77	A	W	65–64
1/14/85	H	W	78–76
2/10/90	H	L	111–114
1/27/01	H	L	96–98
3/14/04	ACC	W	95–87
2/12/05	H	W	99–92

*ACC Tournament game

luxury of taking out his five starters. The crowd responded to the players' efforts with a standing ovation. Off the bench came John Bilney, Dave Henderson, Jon Robinson, Mark Fothergill, and Dutch Morley to run out the clock. Every Terp scored. This win over Duke was the Terps' third consecutive game against an opponent ranked in the top fifteen.

Five days later, Maryland knocked off North Carolina, ranked number seven, 70–69. The Terps won five of their remaining seven games, finishing first in the conference with an 11–3 record, then moved on to the ACC Tournament in Greensboro. Maryland beat Georgia Tech in overtime (51–49) and Clemson in regulation (91–85) before facing Duke for the third time that season, this time for the ACC championship.

It seldom snows in Greensboro, but it sure did that day. By game time, it was an all-out blizzard, and many fans did not make it to the arena. The airport shut down. (Along with newspaperman Mo Siegel, columnist John Schultz, and Marty Aronoff, one of the country's leading statisticians, I walked to the train station to get home. The four of us had to climb down from the platform and hike through the freight yards to board the snow-hampered train. It didn't help that Siegel had no ticket; we had to sneak him on the train.)

In the ACC championship game, Albert King missed his basket as the clock drew down, and Gminski tipped in the winning shot. Duke power forward Kenny Dennard undercut Buck Williams—with no foul called—and it was over.

Even though this was more than 600 games and twenty-six years ago for me, I can vividly recall Dennard moving in on Buck Williams. It looked like a foul to me, and I said so on the air. King was closer than the spectators—and the refs—and it looked the same to him, too. "It *was* a foul," says King. "I saw it happen. When a person is parallel to the ground and he's on someone else's back, then I consider that a foul."

"I did not undercut Buck Williams," Dennard still protests. "I hope people will take the time to understand the laws of physics. Two strong men, 6'8", pushing each other. A physical chess game. And then of course Buck jumped up in the air. Where was I to go except to go under him? Which made it look like I undercut him. But I didn't! And that's why there was no foul called. I think one of the referees was a physics major in college, so he understood the principles. Of course there was great news and much publicity that Kenny Dennard undercut Buck Williams and there was no foul called, and Duke won the game. But I did not undercut him, and I'm glad I have this chance to set the record straight."

King disappeared immediately after the game. Jack Zane, then the UM sports information director, finally found him in the locker room, sitting on a stool hidden from view inside a running shower, crying. Thanks to Zane's persuasion, King reluctantly agreed to personally accept his MVP award. "That was the hardest moment of my basketball career," King admits. "Having to come out and accept that award after missing my shot and losing the game. Absolutely I was crying. My wife reminds me of this all the time. I told Jack that I wasn't going out to get the award. It meant nothing to me at that moment."

When he finally came forward, a standing ovation from both the Maryland and North Carolina fans followed. "Looking back, I'm glad I accepted that MVP since it was an honor," King says.

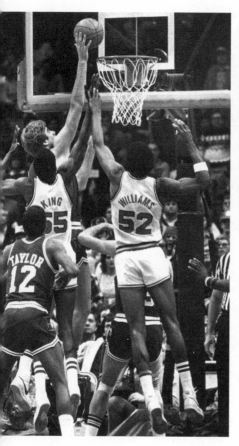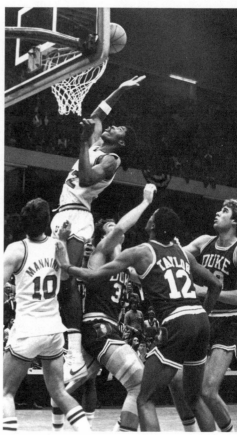

Undercut? Kenny Dennard (33) says no. Buck Williams (52) says yes.

In an 80–68 loss to Duke, January 25, 1986, Len Bias lit up the Blue Devils for 41 points, which still stands as a Maryland road record. Bias had 2 steals, 8 rebounds, and an assist in his thirty-nine minutes on the court. He finished 17 for 17 from the stripe and went 14 for 20 from the field. It was one of his best performances. Afterward, Driesell said that he was "totally confused" that Duke won.

For the Duke contest on March 1, 1995, the Terps traveled to Durham without their coach. Gary Williams was hospitalized with pneumonia, so assistant Billy Hahn took over the coaching reins. I remember kidding Joe Smith in my pregame interview, saying "You'll probably go out and get 45 points."

He got 40.

Duane Simpkins recalls the day: "We went to see Gary in the hospital before we left College Park, and he didn't look good. But Coach Hahn got us settled when we got to Durham. He told us 'Just let it hang out. Play the way you practice.' We knew we had a big game to play, and we brought our best—and so did Duke."

In that game Simpkins went for the winning shot and thought he had made it. "Cherokee Parks was coming at me," Simpkins says. "He's close to 7'0" with those long arms. I flip the ball up and get knocked to the ground. I look up and see the ball go through the net. In a split second I thought—just like the winning shot I had made earlier in the season against Georgetown—that I had done it again. There's going to be a party at College Park, and I'll be the hero."

Then it occurred to Simpkins that no one was jumping on him with congratulations. He yelled, "What the hell happened?" Joe Smith responded, "I won the game." Sure enough, Smith had tapped the ball in after Simpkins went down to the floor.

In game seventeen of the 2004–05 season, Coach Williams brought in a few experts before facing second-ranked Duke in Durham. Steve Blake, Juan Dixon, and Laron Profit visited practice that week and gave the current Terps a few lessons. They talked about having fun, about believing in themselves, and about giving a full effort against the undefeated Blue Devils.

Junior Nick Caner-Medley had 25 points before leaving with an ankle injury. Travis Garrison and Ekene Ibekwe finished off the Blue Devils at the stripe in a 75–66 victory. Ibekwe gave the Terrapins the lead for good with a tough layup in traffic off an inbounds play, set up during a time-out by the coach. Ibekwe's bucket made it 66–64 with 1:23 left. Duke's Daniel Ewing missed badly on a three-point shot, and Garrison started a parade at the line for the Terps. Garrison was 5 for 6 in the final minute, and Ibekwe was 4 for 4 to close it out.

Going into the 2006–07 season, Maryland had won five of the previous eight games against Duke. We all look forward to watching future Duke-Maryland matchups, as the tradition of one of the great rivalries in college basketball continues.

Adrian Branch in OT

It would be the Terps final home game of the 1981–82 season. After defeating thirteenth-ranked Wake Forest 61–56, followed by victories over Duke and Hofstra, Lefty Driesell's team had hit a wall, losing to second-ranked North Carolina (59–56), falling at Clemson (75–66), and then getting knocked off at Wake by the Deacons (48–46).

At Cole Field House on February 24, the Terps dropped their fourth in a row—the longest losing streak of the season—this time to NC State, 52–38. So when the nation's number one team, the Virginia Cavaliers, brought a fifteen-game winning streak to Cole on February 27, every Maryland fan had to be wondering what magic Driesell could conjure to pull off the upset of the season.

The Terps had played Virginia tough in Charlottesville in January, losing by only 5 points in overtime. In that game, Maryland had let a 12-point lead slip away in the second half. Nevertheless, Driesell always had a way of getting his team to play over and above what was expected of them when it mattered.

In February Driesell needed offense, and Adrian Branch would kick his play into high gear for the second game against Virginia. The eighteen-year-old freshman—packing 185 pounds on a 6'7" frame—had come to Maryland from DeMatha High School, just a few miles down Route 1, where he played for legendary coach Morgan Wooten.

Driesell recalls today: "I didn't think we could beat Virginia just by running up and down the court with them. Adrian was a great one-on-one player, and we ran this play we called Drop. We would just give Adrian the ball in middle court, and everybody else was on the baseline, and the two inside guys got rebound positions in case he missed. I did not think Virginia would have anyone that could guard Adrian, and I was right. They could not guard him. They never went to a zone defense. Nobody could stop him.

"So we played one-on-one with Adrian the whole game. I think we were the first team to ever do that, but now many teams do. Virginia ended up first that season, and we were the only team that beat them."

Branch's game stats were impressive: He made 12 of 17 field goals and 5 of 6 free throws, in the process scoring 29 of the team's 47 points (a career high). Although Branch had made big shots in the past for both Maryland and DeMatha, none was bigger than his 15-foot jumper at the foul line—over the outstretched arms of Jeff Jones—as time expired. His shot gave the Terps a 47–46 victory in overtime. The Cole sellout crowd of 14,500 erupted as the horn sounded.

Talk about a guy feeling it and having the hot hand! Branch was virtually unstoppable. Many feel that his February 27 game is one of the greatest individual performances in Maryland history.

Even though Branch scored 29 against the top-ranked Cavaliers, two other Terps played key roles in the upset. Herman Veal sent the game into overtime (tied at 44) with his buzzer-beater at the end of regulation, and sophomore Mark Fothergill frustrated Virginia's 7'4" All-America Ralph Samson, banging with "Big Ralph" the entire game. Sampson took only 5 shots, making 1, and wound up with only 11 points in the game. Not exactly the numbers expected from an All-American.

As reported by Pete Bielski in the *Diamondback*, the student newspaper, Fothergill said, "I was talking to Ralph the whole game, trying to take his mind off the game. Ralph started talking dirty to me, talking trash. That's bush league for the number one player in the country. He has to learn to handle himself." In postgame comments, Sampson called Maryland "a dirty team" and "a crazy team."

Fortunately, Maryland was also the winning team. The Terps held the ball for the last 4:10 of the game. Looking back today, Driesell recalls that he wanted Branch to land the final shot: "We wanted him to take almost every shot. We ran what we called a double-post delay. We would just hold the ball or kick it around. It is tough for a team to steal the ball. We did not have a shot clock back then. And when we felt they were getting tired of chasing it, we would yell "Drop" and give the ball to Adrian in the middle of the court. He'd been pretty tough, so we just called the same play we'd be running at the end, and Adrian made the winning shot."

When Branch came out of DeMatha, Driesell saw something in the left-hander that would make him a terrific college player. Branch graduated the same year as Michael Jordan, and the two even played each other in the McDonald's All-Star Game their senior year. Jordan scored 30 points, Branch 24; Branch received the MVP award that day.

Did Driesell ever imagine that Branch would become one of the all-time leading scorers in Maryland history with 2,017 points? Driesell, who knew that Branch was All-Met at DeMatha and could have written his own ticket at almost any college, says, "A lot of schools, like Michigan, were after him, and it was a recruiting coup that we got him. He and Dutch Morley were the only recruits we got from DeMatha, and you never really know who is going to be great. But I had an idea that he would be." As a Terp, Branch is fourth all-time in scoring, trailing Juan Dixon (2,690), Len Bias (2,149), and Albert King (2,058).

As with any All-American, Branch couldn't do it alone. He had a great supporting cast during his playing days under Driesell: Veal, Fothergill, Keith Gatlin, Jeff Baxter, Derek Lucas, Ben Coleman, Jeff Adkins, and Len Bias. Bias, who was one year behind Branch, would tie Coleman's average 15.3 scoring lead in Branch's junior year. The 1983 Terps were victorious in beating Duke in the ACC final, giving Driesell his only ACC Tournament title.

After Maryland, Branch was drafted in the second round by the Chicago Bulls. He went on to win a world championship with the Los Angeles Lakers in 1987, counting Magic Johnson and Kareem Abdul-Jabbar as teammates. Today Branch is a well-respected motivational speaker at school assemblies, colleges, correctional facilities, and other venues.

He views that Maryland-Virginia game as "individually, my best and the most memorable game of my Maryland career. Virginia was number one. It was the home crowd. Everyone played well. Mark Fothergill was always a very good player; although a lot of times, you didn't realize that. He *came* to play Virginia. Six-foot-nine, 230 pounds. Moreover, he was an irritant to Ralph Samson that day. Dutch Morley controlled the game, set the tempo, and put me in the position to do what I did—which was just score."

When asked if he sensed that Virginia came in with cocky swagger that day, Branch says, "Of course. Being number one, and outside of Michael Jordan they had the top player in the nation in Ralph Sampson. However, with all that said, Virginia did not hold a psychological advantage over us because we were not afraid of them."

Branch was confident in his final shot even though time was running down. He says he felt like he had all the time in the world. "I was so comfortable," he recalls. "One of the biggest things I did was lean in. On the road they might have called it an offensive foul. But not at home." Over the years, Branch has teased Jeff Jones—currently head coach at American University—about that final shot. But today he agrees that "as a competitor you're always the best when you are not afraid, and the best players will always bring the best out of you."

Asked how it feels to be considered one the greatest players in Maryland history, Branch is modest: "I am humbled to be among those like Bias, Elmore, Lucas, McMillen, Walt Williams, Joe Smith, Steve Francis, Juan Dixon . . . and the list goes on."

Just to be remembered seems good enough for Branch.

Lenny Bias

Len Bias signed his agreement to play for Maryland a mile south of campus, at Northwestern High School. He had recently scored 23 points with 15 rebounds to lead his eighth-ranked team to a 101–61 victory over Eleanor Roosevelt High School, clinching the Prince George's County AA championship. His commitment to attend Maryland allowed many Terp fans to breathe a sigh of relief, as NC State was also in serious pursuit of his services, especially his 42-inch vertical jump.

The Maryland faithful knew that Bias wanted to play for UM, as he had gone to Driesell's summer camps. Moreover, with Bias at Maryland, his Landover, Maryland, family would be able to see "Frosty" (the nickname conferred by his mom, Lonise) play at nearby Cole. Driesell, who always called him Leonard, confirmed Bias's desire to win an ACC championship. These were some of the reasons for coming to UM that Bias cited at the packed press conference. He was able to accomplish all those goals before he died, but not his loftiest—playing in the NBA.

I was able to snag a one-on-one radio interview with Bias after the press conference to talk about how hard the decision to come to Maryland was—or wasn't. Bias provided a typical eighteen-year-old's responses of "yes" and "no," with lots of nodding. I had to remind him that the broadcast was for radio.

"You have to talk, Lenny," I suggested.

"Yes, Mr. Holliday," he politely agreed.

By his senior year, this same player had matured and was one of the best interviews on the team.

* * *

Bias got off to a surprisingly quiet start as a freshman, averaging only 7 points a game. One of the reasons he didn't score high— even though he played thirty games—was that Driesell had a heck of a team; it included Ben Coleman, Adrian Branch, Herman Veal, and Jeff Atkins. However, one early game against Georgia Tech gave Terp fans a glimpse of things to come. On February 5, 1983, Bias stung the Yellow Jackets with a season-high 19 points off the bench, giving Driesell thirty-two solid minutes. As impressive as Bias was offensively against Georgia Tech, on defense he rejected one of Mark Price's field goal

attempts with such force that the officials almost had to ask for a new ball.

It was Maryland's seventh consecutive victory. Amazingly they still weren't in the top twenty.

Bias's improvement by sophomore year was astounding. He more than doubled his scoring average, shooting over 55 percent from the field. He also began listening to his teammates regarding his work ethic and improving his all-around play. Bias admitted that he always had talent. He reasoned that he could always shoot, always play inside. But he never really worried about the specifics of what he did. He rarely practiced with the intent to make himself better.

When he became more open to the advice of others, he saw his game improve. Branch recalls that "Lenny would get down on himself if he missed his first couple of shots. He then had a tendency to pass up open looks. I would say to him, 'Hey, keep on shooting.' " The advice worked: Bias would become the best shooter on the team.

You couldn't have asked for a better finish to Bias's sophomore season, as he led the Terps to a 74–62 victory over Duke, contributing 26 points himself. This performance gave Maryland its first ACC Tournament title since 1958. It also earned Bias a nice piece of hardware: He was voted the outstanding player of the tournament. Bias went into the tournament determined to show those who had passed him over for first- and second-team All-ACC selections that they had made a huge mistake.

In the off-season between his sophomore and junior years, Bias worked to become more than just a scorer. His ball handling and shot blocking improved dramatically. And his famed "smooth as silk" jump shot developed. At subsequent games, fans began to witness his ability to elevate—as if he were going to jump out of Cole Field House. His performance became startling.

As I broadcast Bias's games, I began thinking, "I'm seeing a very special player here. This guy's unique." Defensively, he could block shots and rebound with the best of them. Offensively, he could beat you hitting the jumper on the outside or by taking the ball to the hoop on the inside. During the 1984–85 season, Bias made third-team All-American. He was also named the ACC Player of the Year, a feat that he would accomplish again as a senior. He is the only Terp who has won the award twice.

Despite Bias's skill and improvements, he gained very little recognition nationwide before his senior year. That was okay with him. He would say that when an opponent knows you're a scorer, then you can expect to be double- and maybe triple-teamed. The opponent might throw a gimmick defense at you—anything to take you out of your game. So it was fine with Bias if people didn't know his talents.

In College Park it was a different story. Many students soon regarded Bias as an idol. Strolling the campus in his fur coat and jeans, he looked like a model right out of GQ.

Driesell (and Terps fans) might have surveyed Maryland's crop of opponents at the time and come to the conclusion that only North Carolina's Michael Jordan was in Bias's league. For those of you who like to compare numbers, Bias topped Jordan's stats across the board in their respective final college years.

The Washington Post's Michael Wilbon wrote, "I saw great players from both the ACC and Big East every night. Jordan. Ewing. Mullin. Sampson. Later on, David Robinson. But Len

Len Bias versus Michael Jordan– Final Year Stats

	Height	Games	Rebounds	Points	NBA Draft/ Team
Bias (UM, 1986)					
	6'8"	322	24	743	2nd pick/ Boston Celtics
Jordan (UNC, 1984)					
	6'6"	311	63	607	3rd pick/ Chicago Bulls

Bias was the most awesome collegiate player of that bunch. That jumper was so pure. I mean, Michael Jordan, at that time, would have killed for that jumper. And Bias was 2 inches taller."

As for the greatest player ever at UM, you'd have to look at the stats. In terms of 30-point-plus games, Bias and Juan Dixon tie with 6 each, whereas Joe Smith had 7 and Walt Williams had 15. For most points in a season, the order is Dixon (735), Bias (743), and then Williams (776). For most points in a career, Bias (2,149) trails Dixon (2,269). Of course, this is strictly by the numbers.

Various insider accounts have promoted the idea that Len became surly, uncooperative, and distant as he found fame on the court. For the record, I knew and interviewed him for four years. I observed him with his friends and teammates. There was no "dual personality." He remained a good-hearted kid with an NBA dream, and I never witnessed anything less than warm generosity and blazing talent. He never "big-timed" anyone that I knew, despite increased demands on his time. Bias's former roommate, Jeff Baxter, agrees: "Lenny commanded respect from everyone and was a wonderful person throughout his days at UM."

The country began to take notice of Bias by his senior year. Driesell, a proven judge of talent who had coached Len Elmore, Tom McMillen, John Lucas, Walt Williams, and Albert King, knew that his "Leonard" was a future NBA superstar.

Bias impressed everyone on February 20, 1986, in North Carolina. The Tar Heels were ranked number one. They had never lost a game at the Smith Center, better known as the "Dean Dome." Driesell had prepared the Terps exceptionally well, reminding them that they had lost to Carolina in their previous game by only 4 points, 71–67.

The Terps trailed by 11 points late in the first half. Then Bias scored 6 straight, and the Terps went into the locker room at the break down by only 5. Also of note in that first half: Bias was a perfect 9 for 9 at the stripe, setting a new school record for most consecutive foul shots made (22).

Referee Stan Rote recalls, "Len made a jump shot, and I thought maybe he had gotten kicked. I wasn't sure, so next time when we had a dead ball, I asked him, 'Were you fouled on that last jump shot?' 'No sir, I wasn't,' he replied. 'It was just a little short.' And then he added with that wide grin, 'You haven't missed many calls today.' "

Lefty shows a little love for Lenny after another great performance. Assistant coach Mel Cartwright is at right. Jerry Wachter/Sports Illustrated

In the second half, the Terps kept pecking away at the Tar Heel lead. Bias appeared to be almost superhuman, bringing the Terps back from a 9-point deficit with 2:58 left. Then, with seconds to go in regulation, Jeff Baxter hit a 20-footer to send the game into overtime. "Nobody was on me, but that was the most important clutch shot I ever hit in college," Baxter recalls.

With 7 seconds left in overtime, Keith Gatlin put Maryland up 75–72 on a pair of free throws. When Carolina failed to get the ball in bounds, the Terps got it back. Gatlin was the triggerman for the inbounds pass. Seeing that Carolina's Kenny Smith had turned his back on him, Gatlin lobbed the ball off Smith's back, caught it, and laid it in for 2 points. Maryland won the game 77–72, handing North Carolina its first loss in the Smith Center.

I had seen athletes make a play like Gatlin's in practice or while they goofed around on the playground, but I had never seen it done in a college game. "That was gutsy," says Baxter. "He would have never been forgiven by Lefty if he had missed that one."

The line for Bias that evening: 35 points, 6 rebounds, 3 steals, 2 blocks, and 3 assists. Not a bad night at the office. All in all, Bias scored 743 points his senior year—the most ever by a Terrapin in a single season. He led the team in free throw percentage, hitting 86 percent at the line. He also led the Terps in rebounding with 224.

At season's end Bias was selected second in the NBA draft, by the Boston Celtics. With an added Reebok endorsement, he was set for life financially. Bias's NBA dreams would never become reality, however. His tragic death from cocaine poisoning stunned the nation. "Len's death was felt all the more closely because Bias had never left the embrace of his friends and community and seemed to draw strength from them as his success and fame grew," the *Washington Post* reported on June 20, 1986. "His world could be described as a small circle on the map of metropolitan Washington, a circle only as wide as the few miles from his house to the University of Maryland, which he chose to attend so he could remain near his family."

Reflections on Len Bias

"Len Bias was the first player I saw who made me feel like he was from where I was from. Len made me see that playing basketball could be a reality for me. He could play basketball and could be a hero. It wasn't his points as much as his impact on the community."

—Walt Williams

"Maryland has honored Coach Driesell and Coach Gary Williams on more than one occasion. What happened to Len Bias—the good and the illegal—must not be forgotten. The university should be, as Coach Driesell said, proud of Len. This, the twentieth anniversary of his unfortunate death, must be noted."

—Deborah Simmons, *Washington Times,* February 24, 2006

On the morning of June 23, a private funeral was held for close family and friends at the University of Maryland Memorial Chapel. It was standing room only with no media allowed. Driesell, Maryland chancellor John B. Slaughter, the Reverend Leamon W. White of the Mount Bethel Baptist Church, and Richard E. Watkins of AME Church made tearful remarks. Bias's sister Michelle sang "Come Ye Disconsolate."

Bias's mother, Lonise, asked me to sing "The Lord's Prayer" from the choir loft. It was unbearably difficult to get through that song. When I finished, Lonise blew me a kiss, and I went to pieces.

At a public ceremony held at Cole the evening before the family funeral, the Reverend Jesse Jackson asked the mourners to look at Bias's life in the broader view. "God's called him for a higher purpose, to get the attention of this generation and save it," said Jackson. Bias's mother also addressed the crowd: "If you want to see him again, try to live like he lived, in humility and love, and we will never have to cry again."

Billy, Walt, and Keith

I have already singled out Adrian Branch and Lenny Bias in these pages as exemplary Terps—players who carved a place for themselves in Maryland basketball history. Here are three more whose names are familiar to the Terps faithful: Billy Jones, who broke the ACC color barrier; Walt Williams, who scored 30 points or more in seven consecutive games; and Keith Booth, who led his team to four consecutive NCAA Tournaments and later returned to coach at his alma mater.

Billy Jones

On December 4, 1953, seven universities—Clemson, Duke, North Carolina, North Carolina State, South Carolina, Wake Forest, and Maryland—formed the Atlantic Coast Conference. In 1964 Maryland coach Bud Millikan recruited Billy Jones and Pete Johnson, two African-American freshmen, to College Park. Johnson faced some academic problems early on. And so it was Jones who made history as the first African-American basketball player in the ACC in 1965. Fewer than 250 black students attended Maryland when Jones suited up.

"I knew Billy needed an education, and I knew he could play basketball, " recalls Millikan. It was that simple.

Today, Jones is director of cast services at Walt Disney World. His Terp memories are vivid: "The problems [of being an African-American player then] were felt as much off the court as on. There were places we'd go—South Carolina, for example—where I never felt the freedom to do what I wanted to do. We're talking early 1960s, and I could see the gestures and the looks on people's faces in the South. There was never a black face in the stands. I couldn't always hear the words, but I knew what they were saying. People would make racial comments to me with no fear of retaliation or anxiety about what I might do. I had to block all that out and focus on my game. Sometimes it was tough."

In the face of such racial hostility, Jones became more resolute to do his best. "When I came to College Park, I was so used to winning," he says. "I think these people didn't realize how their bias would impact me in a positive way—that it would make me an even stronger person. When people try to deny you what you want to be, then you become more determined."

Jones's teammates—including Joe Harrington, Bill Ward, Rich Drescher, and a lean point guard from Collingswood, New Jersey, named Gary Williams—always stood up for him. "From day one in College Park, my team was there for me," says Jones. He remembers Williams as "the toughest player by far in our pickup games. He played hard. There was no letup."

In 2006 Williams told *Washington Post* reporter Michel Wilbon that he arrived in Maryland a bit uninformed about racial tensions: "I didn't know Maryland and the ACC had been all white. I grew up in southern Jersey," Williams said. "I had always played against black kids. The thing there was you went looking for the best games."

In the South he found a much different situation. For Paul McMullen's 2002 book *Maryland Basketball*, Williams recounted a specific example of discrimination off the courts: "One [experience] that shook us up came after we played at Duke. We went from the gym to the train station in Durham. There was a line where blacks ordered food, and another for whites. That was the first time I had ever seen that. Not that we were heroes, but we all left. Billy Jones never got the credit he deserved, because when Dean Smith retired, everyone made it seem like he broke the ACC racial barrier with Charlie Scott. Billy might have been the first black person in the South Carolina gyms who wasn't sweeping the floors."

Jones sets the record straight on the night he and Williams "snuck into" Cole Field House in 1966 to see Texas Western start five black players and subsequently beat an all-white Kentucky squad for the NCAA Championship. (That historic game—in which sports history intersected with racial equality—was the inspiration for the 2006 Jerry Bruckheimer film *Glory Road*.) "Gary's version of that story [in which he says that both players snuck in] is a little twisted," Jones declares. "I was actually hosting a recruit that day, so I was *supposed* to be there for the game. It was Gary who slipped in with the crowd. And he sat behind the Texas bench."

Despite the fact that many of his games were tinged with racial overtones, some of Jones's fondest memories are of basic plays that simply got the job done.

"The thing about playing for Maryland is this," explains Jones. "We lost more than what we cared to lose. We didn't do as well as we wanted. I was somewhat frustrated in my senior year. But the game that really sticks out in my mind was against South Carolina at Cole in '68. We made two very nice plays—two steals and got fouled on the breakaways—and beat them 66–65. Pete Johnson and I made some plays down the stretch. We pulled it out in the end and did what we had to do. A great ball game all the way down the line. That's the one I remember best."

Walt Williams

Walt "The Wizard" Williams remains one of the most versatile players in the history of the Maryland basketball program. From 1989 to 1992, he was the focal point of every opponent's defense. At the time, the Terps did not have a strong cast of supporting characters. Still, Williams was able to get his shots off and score—almost at will—despite being double- and triple-teamed. His loyalty to Maryland was one of the key reasons the Terps were able to field competitive teams during his tenure.

A native of Temple Hills, Maryland, Williams played for Crossland High School. He stood 6'1" in ninth grade and gained 2 inches a year to reach 6'7" by the time he was a high school senior. He was 6'8" when he entered Maryland. Williams was a Georgetown fan early on, admiring players such as Patrick Ewing, John "Bay-Bay" Duran, and Sleepy Floyd. "But this all changed when Len Bias and Adrian Branch hit the Maryland courts," says Williams. "After Lenny came, I was sold on going to Maryland."

Williams's other school consideration was Temple. "But they practiced too early in the morning," he admits.

In Williams's first season at UM, playing for Coach Bob Wade, the team went 9–11, and Williams averaged 7.0 points per game. Despite the meager record, Williams says his relationship with Wade was very special: "I was a little bitter with the situation when Coach Bob Wade was fired because he meant a lot to me. My mom and dad felt very comfortable with him, and he reminded me of my grandfather. I gave leaving Maryland some thought when Wade left, but, honestly, I didn't agonize over it. I found myself waking up each morning feeling like the Terps is where I belonged. The team was tight—on and off the court—and it felt like family. "

Coach Gary Williams improved the record to 19–14 the next year, but a game against Duke on January 8, 1991, proved to be a crusher for Walt. "You get injuries all the time," he says. "In the first half against Duke, I knew something was seriously wrong with my leg, but I thought I had a charley horse. But the pain became too sharp to be just that, so I asked our trainer at halftime to tape it real tight at the top and bottom of my leg. I didn't give him a chance to look at it, and I went ahead and finished the game."

The Wizard later discovered that his leg was broken; he missed the subsequent eleven games. People thought that he might miss the entire season, but he worked hard to rehabilitate his injury, and he felt ready for Wake Forest at Cole on March 5.

He didn't have 100 percent strength in his leg, but the trainers thought that he wouldn't reinjure it if he played. Walt himself believed that the pain was manageable. "Gary didn't play me in the first half, and we really didn't discuss my coming back," he recalls. "But at halftime I went to Coach and told him that I didn't suit up just to sit on the bench, so he put me in."

Maryland defeated Wake Forest 77–66.

When asked about his relationship with his coach, the Wizard responds: "You know, I wasn't concerned about establishing a personal relationship with the coach. I know I respected him, but I didn't feel like I needed to befriend Gary, nor did he want that with me. I understood his desire to bring the best out in each player, so I gravitated toward the players. I wanted to be a leader for the team. I wanted to be there for them as someone they could turn to, could talk with. When you concentrate on your team like this, I think it tends to separate you from the coach. Gary Williams' coaching style is in your face. He's constantly challenging you. That can rub players the wrong way sometimes."

But coach and player definitely respected each other. Walt says, "I was ready to follow him in any lead he wanted me to go. And whatever he wanted us to do, I wanted to be in a position to

The Wizard works his magic against the Blue Devils.

relay that to the team. He wanted us to play as a unit, and at that time, he needed us to overachieve because we were undertalented compared to the other teams in the league."

Coach Williams moved Walt from forward to shooting guard in his senior year. "It was after a Duke game," Walt confirms. "Duke was running and jumping at me as soon as I would come across half-court. I had eleven turnovers, and we just couldn't get into our offense. Gary felt like it would be tough for opponents to stop me from scoring if I could come in from the wing."

When you talk about stopping the Wizard from scoring, you only need to look at his 1992 record of seven straight games of 30 points or more: 30 at NC State, 32 at North Carolina, 30 and 38 against Florida State, a career-high 39 against Wake Forest, 31 against Clemson, and 33 at Virginia. You might ask if Walt found such accomplishments easy.

"I took one game at a time," he says. "During the games, when you're playing, you don't keep track of these things. The scoreboard wasn't up there letting you know how many points were individually made, and I wasn't talking with the statisticians during my plays. So most of the time I never realized I had over 30 points until after the games were over. I give a lot of credit to my teammates. If they didn't get me the ball, I couldn't have done anything. You can't do it by yourself. It might look like it sometimes, but trust me, it's not."

Going into a February 1992 game against Georgia Tech, Walt was one game shy of tying the all-time ACC record—held by Wake Forest's Lennie Chappell—for most consecutive 30-point games. "That was the first game I went into, worried about getting 30 points," Walt says.

His streak ended with 20 points against Tech. Nevertheless, his legacy is enduring. Says Gary Williams: "Without Walt Williams, the Maryland program would probably have never gotten to where it is now. Walt kept the people coming to games at Cole Field House. He was a great showman. He still has the record for scoring over 30 points in seven straight ACC games. He had to be a great athlete to do this, because it gets very tiring to stay open."

It was special when they honored Walt's number, 42—now hanging in the rafters of Comcast—during his senior year. "I played this game for my father," Walt says. "It was very emotional for me that he could be there to see that."

The Sacramento Kings drafted Williams after graduation. In his rookie NBA year, he donated $125,000 to establish a Walt Williams Sr. scholarship at Maryland, in honor of his dad—a fabulous gesture of giving back to the community. "It's been satisfying to see the looks on the faces of the students who received these scholarships," says Walt. "I hope my legacy—besides the high socks I wore—would be the desire to be the best you can. I owe a lot of credit to my teammates who helped me. The University of Maryland community has always been here for me, and I love 'em to death."

Keith Booth

Baltimore native Keith Booth played junior high basketball in Charm City. Booth saw his first Terps game then—against Louisiana State—courtesy of his coach, who rewarded his best players by sharing his Terps season ticket seats.

Booth never dreamed that he would be playing at Maryland years later. But he did play—leading the Terps to four NCAA Tournaments, including a pair of Sweet Sixteen appearances, and finishing his remarkable college career among UM's all-time leaders in scoring (eighth, 1,776 points), rebounding (sixth, 916), steals (fifth, 193), and free throws made (first, 576). Booth is one of the fifteen players to have their jerseys honored above the Terps home court at the Comcast Center. It's generally agreed that few players worked as hard as he did.

"I had to," Booth says. "I was only 6'6" and was taught that if you want to be effective on the court, being one of the smaller guys, you had to be aggressive and hit guys before they hit you. I had to do it every day and improve every time out. I took it very seriously."

Booth was a first-round selection of the Chicago Bulls in the 1997 pro draft. When the Bulls won the 1998 NBA title, he became only the second player (after Gene Shue) in Terps history to play for a world championship NBA team. Booth says that the two toughest players he ever went up against were both in practice: "Joe Smith at Maryland and Michael Jordan with the Bulls."

Keith Booth (22) lays it up over two defenders.

Fans root for Keith Booth in a big way. *UM Athletic Department*

Booth returned to Maryland in 2004 to become assistant coach. Upon introducing him, Gary Williams had these words of praise: "Keith Booth was the most important recruit during my years here in terms of getting our basketball program to the national level. Keith always achieved success against larger opponents, and his competitive attitude will carry over to our players."

Booth's main challenge as a young coach—not that much older than the students—is to provide the necessary focus for his players. "They have to come in with an open mind, ready to learn," Booth says. "Times are different now than when I played ten years ago, because of the information technology and things that the kids are exposed to and can take advantage of. At the same time, they need to learn how to take things one day at a time and steadily improve." Booth says that these are important lessons for life—both on and off the court.

Greatness by the Numbers

Maryland Athletics honors outstanding Terrapin players by emblazoning their jersey numbers on banners hanging from the rafters of the Comcast Center. The following nine Terps are among the great players who called College Park home:

Bosey Berger, #6

Louis "Bosey" Berger—who was Maryland's first basketball All-American—is regarded as one of the greatest and most likable Maryland athletes. Berger was a Baltimore native but attended McKinley Tech High School in Washington, D.C. Nicknamed "Bosey" by his grandmother, he was a two-time All-America selection and a consensus pick in 1932. His selection is considered a coup, because Maryland was a small agricultural school at the time and not among the athletic giants. Berger was also considered one of the best all-around players of his time.

Berger led Maryland to the 1931 Southern Conference championship, averaging a conference-high 19.1 points over the

nine-game conference season. After graduation, he switched sports, signing a professional contract with the Cleveland Indians. He played in the major leagues for six years with the Indians, Chicago White Sox, and Boston Red Sox. Berger left baseball with a .236 lifetime batting average.

Louis "Bosey" Berger, the Terps' first star player.

Gene Shue, #25

Baltimore native Gene Shue, the Terps' first high-profile basketball star, played for Coach Bud Millikan the first season Cole opened its doors. Shue earned Converse and Helms Foundation All-America honors as a senior while averaging 21.8 points a game. He scored 654 points in 1953, including 40 points against Wake Forest in the 1953 Southern Conference Tournament.

"At Maryland we played the kind of offense where it was all patterns. Very good patterns, where you made numerous passes while looking for opportunities to take a shot," explains Shue. Today, he jokes that he scored 40 points against Wake Forest because he was the only one on the team who could shoot.

The school record-holder in career scoring until 1974, Shue was the third player selected in the 1954 NBA draft. Chosen by the Philadelphia Warriors, Shue was All-Pro twice and a five-time

GENE SHUE
6'2" Forward, Baltimore, Maryland
All-American 1953, 1954

Year	Games Played	Points–Average
1951–52	21	224–10.6
1952–53	23	508–22.1
1953–54	30	654–21.8
Career	74	1,386–18.7

NBA All-Star during his ten-year career with the Warriors, New York Knickerbockers, Ft. Wayne/Detroit Pistons, and Baltimore Bullets. He enjoyed a successful career as a head coach in the NBA with the Washington Bullets, Philadelphia 76ers, and San Diego/Los Angeles Clippers and was twice named the NBA Coach of the Year. As coach and later general manager of the 76ers, Shue led his team to the NBA finals in 1976, where they were defeated by Bill Walton's Portland Trail Blazers.

Of his Maryland days, Shue says that when you played for Millikan, you had to have pride in your defense. Shue's primary focus in the NBA and as a coach was to set a foundation for the team. And Shue's foundation, like Millikan's, was defense. "I took all the defensive principles that I learned from Bud on to the professional level. Often I ran the patterns in the NBA that I learned from Bud. What Bud taught me became instinctual," says Shue.

Len Elmore, #41

Len Elmore is the best rebounder in Maryland history and one of the nation's best ever. His rebounding prowess earned him a spot on most 1974 All-America squads along with offensive-minded teammates Tom McMillen and John Lucas. Elmore is the only player in UM history with more than 1,000 career rebounds (1,053). His 412 rebounds and 14.7 average in 1974 are school records, and his career rebounding average of 12.2 rebounds a game is also the Maryland record. He was a three-time All-ACC selection, Maryland MVP in 1973, and Maryland's Outstanding Senior in 1974.

Len Elmore goes high for the rebound.

LEN ELMORE
6'9" Center, Springfield Gardens, New York
All-American 1974

Year	Games Played	Assists	Rebounds– Average	Points– Average
1971–72	32	37	351–11.0	347–10.8
1972–73	26	35	290–11.2	261–10.0
1973–74	28	48	412–14.7	409–14.6
Career	86	120	1,053–12.2	1,017–11.8

Elmore was selected in the first round of the 1974 NBA draft by the Washington Bullets, but he chose to sign with the Indiana Pacers of the American Basketball Association. He spent ten seasons in the ABA and NBA with the Pacers, Kansas City Kings, Milwaukee Bucks, New Jersey Nets, and New York Knicks.

On leaving professional basketball, Elmore enrolled in Harvard Law School. He graduated in 1987, becoming the first former pro basketball player to graduate from that prestigious school. Today, in addition to his New York City law practice, he is widely known and respected as one of the top college basketball analysts on TV.

Tom McMillen, #54

Tom McMillen averaged 20.5 points and 9.8 rebounds during his three-year career at Maryland and was a three-time All-American and three-time Academic All-American. He is one of only two players in school history with a career scoring average of more than 20 points per game.

McMillen led Maryland to the 1972 National Invitation Tournament championship, earning tournament MVP honors. He also earned a silver medal for the United States in the 1972 Olympic Games. After college McMillen put his professional basketball career on hold for one year in order to take advantage of a Rhodes scholarship, which enabled him to study at Oxford. "I worked hard to become Maryland's first Rhodes scholar," he says.

TOM MCMILLEN
6'11" Forward, Mansfield, Pennsylvania
All-American 1972, 1973, 1974

Year	Games Played	Assists	Rebounds– Average	Points– Average
1971–72	32	33	306–9.6	667–20.8
1972–73	29	28	284–9.8	616–21.2
1973–74	27	41	269–10.0	524–19.4
Career	88	102	859–9.8	1,807–20.5

Future congressman Tom McMillen fires his patented "J."

McMillen played in the NBA for eleven seasons with the Buffalo Braves, Atlanta Hawks, New York Knicks, and Washington Bullets. In 1986 he was elected to the U.S. Congress from Maryland's Fourth District; he served three terms. Today, McMillen is a successful businessman living in Washington, D.C. He says that his greatest Terp memory is from his last game against Virginia in 1974: After the buzzer, fans lifted him and Len Elmore in celebration and carried them around Cole.

John Lucas, #15

A three-time All-American who is considered by many the greatest guard in the history of the Terps program, John Lucas was the first Maryland player to earn first-team All-ACC honors in three straight seasons. He is number five on Maryland's all-time scorer list with 2,015 points and number four on the school's all-time assists list.

With Lucas as their point guard, the Terps finished the 1973 season ranked eighth, the 1974 season ranked fourth, and the 1975 season ranked fifth in Associated Press polls. Lucas also was a collegiate All-American in tennis, a sport in which he was a two-time ACC singles champion and a one-time ACC doubles champion. The number one selection in the 1976 NBA draft, Lucas played fourteen seasons in the NBA with the Houston

JOHN LUCAS
6'4" Guard, Durham, North Carolina
All-American 1974, 1975

Year	Games Played	Assists	Rebounds– Average	Points– Average
1972–73	30	178	83–2.8	425–14.2
1973–74	28	159	82–2.9	564–20.1
1974–75	24	91	100–4.2	469–19.5
1975–76	28	86	109–3.9	557–19.9
Career	110	514	374–3.4	2,015–18.3

John Lucas flies through the air to score.

Rockets, Golden State Warriors, Washington Bullets, San Antonio Spurs, Milwaukee Bucks, and Seattle Supersonics.

After his playing days ended, Lucas served as head coach of the San Antonio Spurs (1992–94), the Philadelphia 76ers (1994–96), and the Cleveland Cavaliers (2000–03).

Albert King, #55

One of the most prolific scorers in school history, Albert King averaged double figures during each of his four Terp seasons.

King found early fame as a fourteen-year-old, when he was featured in a 1974 book about Brooklyn, New York, pickup basketball: *Heaven Is a Playground*, by Rick Telander. King had yet to decide on a high school, but he had already received a letter from Lefty Driesell's office at Maryland, urging him to have an enjoyable summer and to fill out a basketball questionnaire. At the time, King "really wanted to just be like everyone else." Among children his own age, he was stared at and pestered. "Basketball, basketball, basketball—that's all I hear," he moaned.

Of interest in the Telander book is an anecdote about King meeting another young standout: Moses Malone (who signed with Maryland but went straight to a pro career after high school). King met Moses at a showcase event for the country's top seniors. "Though only a spectator himself," reports Telander, "Albert was forced into a one-on-one confrontation with Malone. Wearing his street clothes, Albert showed a quickness at least the match of Malone's."

Playing despite a painful thigh injury, Albert King is still able to hit his patented jump shot against North Carolina's James Worthy.

ALBERT KING
6'7" Forward, Brooklyn, New York
All-American 1980, 1981

Year	Games Played	Assists	Rebounds–Average	Points–Average
1977–78	28	64	187–6.7	381–13.6
1978–79	28	62	144–5.1	444–15.9
1979–80	31	86	207–6.7	674–21.7
1980–81	31	92	177–5.7	559–18.0
Career	118	304	715–6.1	2,058–17.4

By the time King came to Maryland, he was regarded as the nation's top high school recruit, having averaged 38.6 points and 22 rebounds as a high school senior. A great cast of characters— Buck Williams, Greg Manning, Dutch Morley, Reggie Jackson, and Ernest Graham—soon surrounded him. "That crew we had were very good teammates, and the thing was that nobody seemed to have an ego," says King. "We all tried to work together *to give Albert King the ball.*"

No other class in the history of Maryland basketball had four players drafted into the NBA—King, Williams, Manning, and Graham.

King ranks as the number three all-time Maryland scorer with 2,058 career points. His career scoring average of 17.4 points per game is the sixth best in UM history. His 38 points versus Clemson in 1980 is a Terp record in ACC Tournament games. King shared the 1981 team MVP award with Buck Williams after winning the award outright in 1980. He was the ACC Player of the Year in 1980 and a first-team All-ACC selection again in 1981.

King cites as his best game the 1980 ACC finals matchup against Clemson. "I like to try and do more than score, and that game gave me a chance to rebound, pass, and score," he says.

The top-seeded Terps beat Clemson but lost to sixth-seeded Duke 73–72. The latter game ended after Kenny Dennard undercut Buck Williams with no foul call on the final play.

King was picked in the first round—the tenth pick overall—of the NBA draft by the New Jersey Nets. He spent nine NBA seasons with the Nets, Philadelphia 76ers, San Antonio Spurs, and Washington Bullets. His brother, Bernard, is also a former NBA star and league scoring champion.

King says that one Terp who doesn't get mentioned much these days is the late Taylor Baldwin. "He was a crowd favorite and a good defender with a nice hook shot. Whenever Taylor popped a shot, the crowd went wild."

Today, King is a successful businessman who owns several Wendy's fast-food franchises. He enjoys telling his son about his Terp experiences, pointing to other alums who also benefited from the University of Maryland experience. "You really don't appreciate it sometimes when you're playing, the learning and the maturing," says King. "But I think back to Cole—coming through that tunnel—and how great the players and Coach Lefty were. Lefty was in a league by himself as far as personality was concerned. I probably helped him go bald, but it was all great fun."

King believes that it is great to look back but more important to enjoy the experience while you're going through it. "That's what I tell players today," he says. "That's the key."

Buck Williams, #52

An outstanding scorer and extraordinary rebounder, Buck
Williams earned All-America honors following his junior season
and entered the NBA directly afterward. He averaged 15.5 points
and 11.7 rebounds a game as a junior. He is the number four
rebounder in Maryland history with 928 career rebounds. His
career average of 10.9 rebounds a game is second best in school
history. Williams also averaged double-figure scoring in each of
his three seasons while registering the school's best-ever career
field goal shooting percentage: 61.5 percent.

Williams led the ACC in rebounding as a freshman in
1978–79, ranked third in 1979–80, and ranked second in
1980–81. He was a member of the 1980 Olympic team that did
not compete in the Moscow Olympic Games.

BUCK WILLIAMS
6'8" Center/Forward, Rocky Mount, North Carolina
All-American 1981

Year	Games Played	Assists	Rebounds–Average	Points–Average
1978–79	30	18	332–10.8	300–10.0
1979–80	24	27	242–10.1	371–15.5
1980–81	31	31	363–11.7	482–15.5
Career	85	76	928–10.9	1,153–13.6

Terrapin Buck Williams brought honor to College Park when he played on the 1980 U.S. Olympic team.

Williams applied for a hardship waiver into the NBA draft in 1981 and was selected number three overall, by the New Jersey Nets. He was named the NBA Rookie of the Year in 1982 and eventually played eighteen pro seasons with the Nets, Portland Trail Blazers, and New York Knicks.

Joe Smith, #32

The consensus 1995 Naismith Collegiate Player of the Year, Joe Smith was named the Atlantic Coast Conference Player of the Year and a UPI third-team All-American as a freshman in 1994. He became one of only three sophomores in the history of the conference to earn player of the year honors, joining NC State's David Thompson and Virginia's Ralph Sampson.

Smith was an All-ACC first-team selection in both his freshman and sophomore seasons. He averaged 20.1 points and 10.7 rebounds over his sixty-four-game career, establishing himself as one of only five players in UM history to average a career double-double. Smith was selected number one overall in the 1995 NBA draft by the Golden State Warriors; he has played for the Warriors, Philadelphia 76ers, Minnesota Timberwolves, Detroit Pistons, and Milwaukee Bucks.

JOE SMITH
6'10" Center/Forward, Norfolk, Virginia
All-American 1994, 1995

Year	Games Played	Assists	Rebounds– Average	Points– Average
1993–94	30	25	321–10.7	582–19.4
1994–95	34	40	362–10.7	708–20.8
Career	64	65	683–10.7	1,290–20.1

Steve Francis, #23

Steve Francis was a second-team All-America selection following his outstanding junior season at Maryland. An All-ACC first-team and ACC All-Tournament first-team selection, he finished fourth in the balloting for ACC Player of the Year in 1999. He was named the Division I Newcomer of the Year by *Sports Illustrated* and was a finalist for the Naismith and Wooden Awards as the collegiate player of the year. Francis also was named to the All-ACC defensive team by the conference coaches.

Francis earned MVP honors at the BB&T Classic in Washington, D.C., as he helped Maryland beat number five–ranked Stanford and NIT participant DePaul. He also was selected to the all-tournament team at the Puerto Rico Shootout. Francis was chosen by the Vancouver Grizzlies as the second overall pick in the first round of the 1999 NBA draft; he later was traded to the Houston Rockets, then to the New York Knicks. He won NBA Co-Rookie of the Year honors in 2000 and was voted an NBA All-Star in 2002.

STEVE FRANCIS
6'3" Guard, Takoma Park, Maryland
All-American 1999

Year	Games Played	Assists	Rebounds– Average	Points– Average
1999	34	152	154–4.5	579–17.0

Steve Francis graced the Terrapin hardwoods for only one year. But, oh, how Stevie could soar and score.
UM Athletic Department

While racking up pro accomplishments, Francis remained connected to Maryland. He was playing a pickup game in Cole in 2000 when a freak tornado moved through College Park, causing extensive damage, killing two students, and clearing a highrise dormitory. Many students were displaced, including Terrapins Earl Badu, Lonny Baxter, Steve Blake, Juan Dixon, and Drew Nicholas. Francis, then a point guard for the Rockets, generously hosted a dinner for the 700 students affected by the storm. Many in attendance that evening had been Terp supporters when Francis helped lead the team two years earlier.

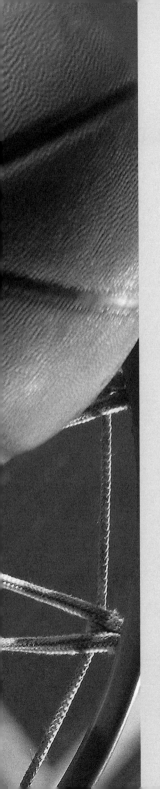

The Greatest Game Ever

You had to be there to fully appreciate the agony of this defeat. It was the finals of the ACC Tournament in Greensboro, North Carolina, on March 9, 1974. Maryland versus North Carolina State. The winner would advance to the NCAA Tournament. Many basketball fanatics and most so-called experts consider this match to be the best collegiate game ever. It certainly is one of the finest in the history of the ACC.

Box Score: 1974 ACC Tournament Final

Name	MP	PT	R	A	PF	TO
Owen Brown	26	14	2	0	5	2
Len Elmore	45	18	13	0	3	2
Billy Hahn	7	0	0	0	1	0
Maurice Howard	45	22	3	5	1	2
John Lucas	45	18	3	10	4	3
Tom McMillen	45	22	7	5	1	5
Tom Roy	12	6	3	0	4	1
Maryland	**225**	**100**	**31**	**20**	**19**	**15**
Tommy Burleson	39	38	13	2	3	1
Mark Moeller	7	0	0	0	0	2
Morris Rivers	42	8	5	1	4	3
Phil Spence	34	7	6	0	2	0
Tim Stoddard	19	4	6	1	1	1
Monte Towe	41	17	2	8	2	1
David Thompson	43	29	5	3	2	6
NC State	**225**	**103**	**37**	**15**	**14**	**14**

MP=minutes played, PT=points, R=rebounds, A=assists, PF=personal fouls, TO=turnovers

Number one–ranked NC State beat Maryland, 103–100, in overtime to win the conference tournament. Six players from the championship game were named All-Americans. Three were Terps: Tom McMillen, John Lucas, and Len Elmore. The Wolfpack had Monte Towe, Tom Burleson, and David Thompson. Thompson received great press at the time as being one of the best players on the court.

"And he certainly was all of that," says Elmore. "I consider Thompson to be one of the three greatest players in the history of college basketball, along with Kareem Abdul-Jabbar and a toss-up between Bill Russell and Oscar Robertson. Thompson was right up there with guys who changed the game."

Thompson presented many matchup problems because of his versatility. He could jump with the big men. "If we put a larger guy on him," says Elmore, "he'd take him outside and go around him. There were times State went to four corners, and I wound him having to guard him because I was the best defensive player on the team. But Thompson had a 42-inch vertical leap. We used to call him 'Luke Skywalker.' " Elmore's praise is obviously on target; Thompson was named player of the year by most major sports organizations in 1975.

But Elmore points to State's Burleson as making the major difference in the game. "When the ball would reverse, Burleson would set up down low. But [with him] at 7'4", and the difference between us in height and reach, there wasn't much I could do to stop him. I think he scored more points in that game than in the rest of his career."

The Terps also had to battle fatigue, as they had played three games in a row, punishing North Carolina the night before by 20 points in one of the worst ACC Tournament losses in the Dean Smith–coached era. That night took its toll on the Terps.

The sensational Thompson had scored 37 points against Virginia in the Wolfpack's semifinal victory against the Cavaliers, 87–66. Maryland coach Lefty Driesell had been trying to figure out some way to contain Thompson when the teams met in Greensboro. Many people thought he might try a box-and-one; Wolfpack coach Norm Sloan certainly hoped so, because when Duke tried the box-and-one against NC State, Thompson scored 40 points. But Driesell was known for his tight man-to-man defense.

The Terps started strong, with a 12-point lead early on. NC State trailed by 5 at halftime.

It turned out that Thompson was not the key to victory. As Elmore points out, it was Burleson who made the difference: He completed 18 of 25 shots from the floor, scored 24 points in the second half alone, and ended with a career game of 38 points. (He had averaged only 18 points a game during the season.) Thompson had scored 29 points by the closing seconds of regulation, when the game was tied at 97.

Maryland had a chance to win it when Maurice Howard got a pass from McMillen on a break and went down the floor. Burleson followed. Howard did not take the shot, passing back out to Lucas, who rushed a shot. Burleson got a piece of it, and time expired. "It's been thirty-one years, but today somebody might have pump-faked and drove to the basket," says Elmore. "John was out at the top of the key, but he wasn't ready to shoot.

Everyone thought Mo was going to take it, and we relaxed."

In overtime Lucas missed a one-and-one that could have put the Terps ahead. Phil Spence came back and nailed an uncontested jumper with 2:04 left in overtime, giving NC State a 101–99 lead. Then the Wolfpack's Towe, the smallest guy on the floor, canned a couple of free throws with 6 seconds left. "We played until the last drop of blood was left on the floor," said Maryland's Tom Roy.

NC State would go on to win the NCAA Tournament, ousting Bill Walton's UCLA team in double overtime in the semifinals and beating Marquette in the final game.

Maryland game stats included 22 points for McMillen and 18 each for Lucas and Elmore. The loss to NC State ended the Terps' twelve-game winning streak, their season, and the McMillen and Elmore era. In their three seasons at Maryland, those two players won seventy-three of the ninety games they played together. "The realization that it was over came [when we were] sitting in the locker room," recalls Elmore. "In postmortem we had to decide whether we would play in the NIT or not. But Tom and I, as captains, knew that we had already won the NIT in our career. So that wouldn't be a major accomplishment doing it again. For us it was really the NCAA or bust."

At the time, the press focused on the Terps' sadness over losing a shot at the championship. Now, Elmore points to the goals accomplished: The team put the Maryland program back on the map and brought it to national prominence.

After the loss, Driesell boarded the NC State team bus, shook hands with all the players, and encouraged them to go ahead and win a national championship. He told Burleson, "That was the greatest game a center has ever played in the ACC. I've never seen a center dominate a game like that." Driesell said that he would vote for NC State to be number one in the final poll, even if that meant Maryland had to be number two.

How would you like to be the number two team in the nation and not be able to play in the NCAA Tournament? That's exactly what happened. The conference rules were different then—a team had to win its conference tournament to make the NCAA Tournament. But Maryland's number four finish in the final Associated Press poll that season helped persuade the NCAA to change the rules a year later. The tournament committee expanded the field from thirty-two to forty-eight teams, which allowed more than one team from a conference.

Elmore laments, "Here we were ranked number four, and State goes on to win the national championship, and we stayed home because we lost to them in overtime. Of a field of thirty-two, you could say we were better than thirty of those teams." Incidentally, Driesell played only seven men.

On the twenty-fifth anniversary of the shootout, *Baltimore Sun* reporter Bill Free noted, "At least the Terps won the battle for the most NBA draft picks, 6–4. John Lucas, Tom McMillen, Len Elmore, Mo Howard, Tom Roy, and Owen Brown were selected in the NBA draft."

In 2002 the ACC announced its fiftieth anniversary team. The Wolfpack had four players, including Burleson and Thompson. Maryland had eight players, including Lucas, Elmore, and McMillen. "Maybe we didn't win a national championship," says Elmore, "but Tom and I were fortunate that we could blend the team with Mo Howard, Tom Roy, John Lucas, Owen Brown, and

Billy Hahn. It was an honor to play with them. Tom and I roomed together, and to find some common ground coming from such different backgrounds is what college basketball is all about. We started in 1970, were inducted in the Hall of Fame together, and we're still close friends. I wonder if any of the other teams have the kind of close relationship we all have today."

Gary's Turning Points

In 1993, and for the previous decade, the Georgetown Hoyas were formidable, with a striking status sealed by their NCAA Championship victory over Houston in 1984. Thanks to coach John Thompson and center Patrick Ewing, the Hoyas became a rousing influence on young, aspiring players nationwide. At the time Thompson told *Washingtonian* magazine, "I want to be a winner. I want my kids to graduate, and I want to get rich."

In *Big Man on Campus*, a biography of Thompson, *Washington Post* sports editor Len Shapiro wrote that the concept known as *bogarting* (as in Humphrey Bogart) "goes a long way in defining John Thompson's philosophy of life. Bogarting means taking control of the situation, walking and talking with arrogant authority, and being prepared to back it up, on and off the basketball court . . . playground power, pure and simple."

Meanwhile, the Maryland Terps were making inroads under new coach Gary Williams, though the team was still struggling to find itself.

The 1993–94 season opener decisively changed Maryland's underdog reputation. The Terps eked out an 84–83 overtime victory over Georgetown, with freshman Joe Smith emerging in style with 9 boards and 26 points. This win would prove to be a critical turnaround for the program—the beginning of eleven consecutive Terp trips to the NCAA Tournament.

Williams describes that Hoya defeat as a milestone: "Sometimes a game springboards your team into a different situation, and that's what that game did for Maryland. We were coming off of three years with sanctions from the NCAA from the previous coaching administration, and we were not considered a very good basketball program at the time. We played Georgetown on their turf at the old US Air Arena. It was the Friday after Thanksgiving, and the game was televised by ESPN, the only basketball game on TV that day."

Georgetown, with Othella Harrington, was ranked fourteenth in the country. Williams started two freshmen (Smith and Keith Booth) and three sophomores (Duane Simpkins, Exree Hipp, and Johnny Rhodes). The Terps were down 14 points in

Duane Simpkins (10) beats the clock and the Hoyas.

the second half. They came back to tie it up and force overtime, and Simpkins won the game with a last-second layup.

Simpkins knew that Maryland had something to prove. He remembers the sequence leading up to his winning bucket: "We forced it to overtime. We were behind 8 points and just chipped it down. Kurtis Schultz—now the strength and conditioning coach for the Tampa Bay Bucs—stole the ball.

"We immediately called a time-out," says Simpkins. "Coach Williams didn't draw up a play for us. He told me to run the clock down, make something happen, and 'try to drop the ball off to Joe if you can.' All I really heard was 'Penetrate to the basket.' I wasn't sure if I would shoot, but I decided to be as aggressive as possible."

Joey Brown was the point guard for Georgetown, a very good defensive player. As Simpkins dribbled the ball, he saw that Brown was in a defensive stance. Brown went left, and Simpkins went right. "It was instinctive," says Simpkins. "I had been working on my floater, so I let it go. When the ball dropped through the net, everyone started jumping around. My thought was 'We've got to get back on defense because there's still time left.' Fortunately, Georgetown couldn't recover, and the rest is history."

Simpkins came over to where I was broadcasting, gave me a high five, and jumped on the table. The place went nuts. It was a major upset.

The first game between the schools after a thirteen-year hiatus was the match that made people—especially Maryland folk—realize that the Terps could be good. Seeing that Maryland would once again have a great program, fan confidence swelled.

The day after the game, *Washington Post* columnist Tony

Kornheiser made the following observation: "Gary Williams has been wanting to play this game since he came to Maryland. Like games against Duke and North Carolina, this is a 'two-suiter' for Williams, the kind where he sweats frenetically through his own clothing, and assistant Billy Hahn's too."

The game was not only a pivotal moment for Williams but also a coming-out party for Smith. "Joe was one those players who was unheralded at the time," Williams explains. "He wasn't a high school All-American or anything, but what he did against Georgetown under that kind of pressure was incredible. He wound up being the ACC Freshman of the Year and in his sophomore year, ACC Player of the Year."

Simpkins recalls: "I was with Coach Williams the day that we learned Keith Booth had chosen Maryland. We were high-fiving each other. Everyone was excited that Keith was coming, but not a word was being said about Joe Smith when he came from Norfolk, Virginia. In preseason we had our first pickup game on a Sunday night, and Joe destroyed all of our big guys, especially Namanja Petrovic.

"The next morning, Namanja said he was transferring. Joe Smith demolished him. He hurt his pride, put him to shame, and by the next week Namanja was gone."

In 1995 Smith became one of only three sophomores to be named ACC Basketball Player of the Year. He was selected number one in the 1995 NBA draft by the Golden State Warriors.

* * *

Another turning point came on February 7, 1995, when the eighth-ranked Terps upset number one–ranked North Carolina at Cole Field House, 86–73.

Coach Williams recalls: "We had a good team in '95, but Carolina was Carolina. If you were to ask people across the country to name two of the top five programs of the past fifty years, probably 95 percent of the folks would pick Duke and North Carolina. Therefore, if you want to be considered on their level, you have to beat them."

Williams adds that he remembers the crowd during that game as much as anything else. "It's commonplace now for the fans to come out on the court after a win, but we were one of the first crowds at that game to do so. I was worried about getting hurt trying to leave the floor."

The next day Kornheiser wrote in the *Washington Post*: "Because no lead is ever safe against North Carolina, Gary Williams didn't allow himself to think the game was over—even when Maryland was up by 10 with less than a minute to go."

Williams told Kornheiser that "once the buzzer went off, six years worth of feelings I'd kept inside raced through me in about ten seconds. I thought about the sanctions, and Len Bias, and how when I got here people felt the basketball team was really hurting the university. And now this was so positive. I felt we'd come 180 degrees . . . I went into the locker room and told the players to enjoy this. 'Enjoy tonight. This is what you play basketball for: to have the opportunity to play the number one team on your home court and beat them.' I wish I could have enjoyed it more myself. But I started thinking about how we might have a letdown against Florida State; I saw what happened to GW at St. Bonaventure." Williams laughs sheepishly. "I told the kids not to be like me—to enjoy this, and not worry so much."

Future Hall of Fame coach Gary Williams. Over Williams's shoulder sits longtime Terp supporter (and onetime team manager) Jack Heise, in necktie. John Biever/Sports Illustrated

* * *

Three years later, on January 14, 1998, Maryland handed the Tar Heels their first loss of the season. It also marked the first Maryland win against coach Bill Guthridge, who had taken over when Dean Smith retired. Terp guard Laron Profit scored 6 points in overtime to lead Maryland to a 93–89 victory. With this win, Williams would go on to defeat six number one teams, more than any other college coach had accomplished.

By the 2000–01 season, the Terps had taken a giant leap forward. The seeding "gods" sent the Terps out west to Boise, Idaho, first to face local neighbors George Mason University. Maryland then defeated Georgia State (coached by Lefty Driesell) and Georgetown before stunning second-ranked Stanford. "Here was our chance for the first time in Maryland basketball history to go to the Final Four," says Williams. "Stanford was the number one seed. We played in L.A., so all the Stanford alums were there. I saw John Thompson sitting with Bill Russell. There were a lot of nerves in the locker room before that game. It was a very tough place for us to play."

In the first two Stanford possessions, Juan Dixon stole the ball and went downcourt to lay it in. After that, Williams was confident that the Terps could win. It turned out to be a relatively easy victory. Stanford's Collins twins (who later played in the NBA) went after Lonny Baxter. At 6'7", Baxter was able to survive and was named the most outstanding player of the tournament's West Region.

Williams considers the win a milestone for the program: "Until you get to the Final Four," he says, "there is a certain ceiling for your program. In other words, until you get to the Final

Four, people do not put you at the same level of the teams who have been there, so this was really a breakthrough win for us."

* * *

After a loss at number one–ranked Duke by 21 points on January 17, 2002, the Terps reeled off thirteen straight victories, including payback time for the Blue Devils. Duke was still perched atop the polls when Maryland upset them 87–83 before a raucous, sellout crowd at Cole—the Terps' eighth win in that streak. "With the Duke win," says Coach Williams, "we did not know it at that time obviously, but we were building toward winning the national championship. Anytime you can beat Duke means you can play with anyone in the country. That win gave us the confidence that we were good enough."

From my broadcaster's seat, it seemed that players didn't come any tougher than the Steve Blake. He had the total package, including a catlike quickness, evidenced by his best play of the game: In a blink of the eye, Blake picked Jason Williams's pocket clean at half-court, while the Duke point guard was taking a glance at his coach for some last-second instructions.

"Steve's play always gets on ESPN whenever they show the top basketball plays," says Coach Williams. "It was a timing play by Blake. Duke's Jason Williams was standing at half-court, waiting to run the last play of the half. We were only up 5 points at the time, and if he scored, it would be a 2- or 3-point game. Instead, Blake steals, scores, and makes it a 7-point game. And we got all the momentum going into the second half. Often, basketball plays are bigger than the 2 points you get from them. That was one of those times."

By March 2002 the Terps were the hottest and most talked-about team in America. The Connecticut Huskies were the only hurdle remaining for the Terps to advance to their second consecutive Final Four. It would be the most electrifying tournament contest of the Terps' postseason run, with Maryland defeating UConn, 90–82, in Syracuse.

Coach Williams recalls the tense final minutes: "We had been to the Final Four the previous season, and we wanted to go back with the same team, but Caron Butler for the Huskies went nuts in the second half with 26 points, and they had us on the ropes. We were down 3. With about two minutes left, it was our possession, and if we had missed and Connecticut scored, it would have been a 5- or 6-point game with less than two minutes left.

"I'm sure that Juan couldn't have seen the basket when he shot—probably with Butler flying at him—but he knew he was going to make it, and he nailed a big three-pointer. UConn then missed, and Steve Blake hit a three-pointer—his only field goal of the game—to put us up, and we gradually took it out to 9 points. That was as competitive a game as I've ever played because the Huskies played very well that day."

I was one of the last people to leave the jubilant locker room after the team knocked off UConn. As I was walking down the hallway, heading for the team bus, Dixon came up from behind and put his arm around my shoulder. "How about that game, Mr. Holliday?" he asked.

I replied, "You took their best shot, and we're going to the Final Four." And for that moment I thought back to the previous year and the feeling of beating Stanford and getting a ticket

The Terps' all-time leading scorer, Juan Dixon.

punched to the Final Four. The mission statement of those guys was a vow to the man that they would be going back.

And there they were. Going back to the Final Four.

Two Great Coaches

When I began broadcasting Maryland basketball in 1979, Charles Grice "Lefty" Driesell was starting the eleventh of his seventeen seasons as head coach at Maryland. Only four coaches had preceded him: H. Burton Shipley (1923–47), Flucie Stewart (1947–50), Bud Millikan (1950–67) and Frank Fellows (1967–69).

Driesell had played ball at Duke, graduating in 1954. He left a coaching job at Davidson College to sign on with Maryland at $21,000 a year, taking over a team that had gone 8–18 the previous season under Frank Fellows.

The first words out of Driesell's mouth were "national champions" as he hyped a new vision for Maryland. "Maryland has the potential to be the UCLA of the East Coast, or I wouldn't be here," he told the press. When asked by a reporter if he was "austere," he replied, "I don't even know what the word means. Let's get back to some country talk."

It was Driesell who made Cole Field House the place to be. He insisted on courtside seating, which increased capacity to 14,500. Longtime UM supporter Jack Heise was instrumental in first approaching Driesell to come to Maryland. "Lefty put the floor seats in to give Cole that atmosphere of excitement and enthusiasm," says Heise, who was present the first day Cole opened and on the night the Terps played their final game there against Virginia. "None of us dreamed what it would go on to be, but we were very proud of the new arena."

Indeed, the seats began to fill. "Hail to the Chief" became Driesell's theme song. His flashing the "V for victory" sign and his angry, stomping foot became the Southern showman's trademarks.

Under NCAA rules Driesell knew that he could begin season practice one minute after midnight on the approved day. On the first day of his first season, he met with his thirteen-man squad of team candidates at 6:30 A.M. on the Byrd Stadium track. He told them to run a mile in less than six minutes. Junior Dick Stodbaugh, a 6'7" forward, posted the fastest time (5:30). Senior Bill Siebenaler was last man over the line at 5:55:9. Driesell thought that this early practice was convenient, given that classes at College Park started at 8:00 A.M.

One season later Lefty decided, "Heck, students don't sleep anyway." Moreover, he thought that if he could begin his team's

Lefty Driesell: Vital Basketball Stats

Born: December 25, 1931, in Norfolk, Virginia

Colleges Coached: Davidson (1960–69); Maryland (1969–86); James Madison (1988–97); Georgia State (1997–2003)

Ranks fifth all-time among Division I coaches with 786 career wins

Coached twenty-two seasons of twenty or more wins

Only coach to win 100 games at four different schools

Shares NCAA record of taking four different schools to the NCAA Tournament

Coached teams to four different conference tournament titles

Won Conference Coach of the Year in four different leagues

Inducted into the University of Maryland, Duke University, State of Virginia, Davidson University, and Granby High School halls of fame

mile run one minute after midnight, it would show the competition that "Maryland was starting practice hours before everyone else was." His gimmick worked. About 100 students showed up on October 15, 1970, to see the Terps run the midnight mile. Thus "Midnight Madness" was born. The next year, it would be 1,000 students showing up. Driesell even added a scrimmage game to the run.

The event soon spread to other campuses. When teachers complained that their students weren't showing up for classes the next day, the NCAA changed the date of the first practice from October 15 to the first Saturday in October.

Driesell's slow-cooked Southern charisma was coupled with sharp, relentless recruiting skills. He usually was in command of his student-athletes and his staff, but occasionally he lost his temper. His first ACC win of the 1986 season, against Wake Forest, nearly ended in a fistfight. A heckler in the stands yelled, "You're still in seventh place," as the Terps beat Wake 77–55. Driesell jumped the rails and took after him. "Go on and push me, and we'll get after it. You start and I'll finish; I'm not afraid of anybody," he bellowed.

Assistant coach Oliver Purnell calmed the old left-hander down. "I ain't a-scared of anybody," Driesell repeated after his blood pressure dropped a few points. "Some guy cussed me, some guy wanted to get his name in the papers. I told him I'd knock his teeth out."

Yet I can recall Driesell sprawled out on the bed, reading the Bible during many road trips. He was very religious. I also recall going to his house the day he was fired from Maryland, after the Len Bias tragedy. He was absolutely distraught that the university held him accountable for Bias's cocaine overdose. I thought then (and still do now) that it was very unfair that Driesell took the heat for the situation. He remains deeply hurt by the university's decision.

That he has participated in many UM events—the closing of Cole Field House and a Comcast Center celebration to mark Gary Williams's status as the winningest coach at Maryland, for example—just goes to show you how decent a man Driesell is. Athletic director Debbie Yow should take credit for her work in extending the olive branch. All of the past administrators who took part in Driesell's dismissal are gone; Yow has worked to welcome Driesell back to his old home.

Driesell's true legacies are the players he recruited and coached and the games he won. Over seventeen years at College Park—averaging 20.5 wins a year—Driesell had eight teams ranked in the top twenty, five in the top ten. He was inducted into the Maryland Athletic Hall of Fame in 2002. Over his entire career, he served forty-one seasons as a head coach and notched the fifth-most wins in Division I history. He is the only coach to have 100 or more wins at four different schools (Davidson, Maryland, James Madison, and Georgia State); his total number of victories stands at 786.

Driesell retired from Georgia State in 2005. The Associated Press reported him as saying, "I woke up New Year's Day, and I told my wife, Joyce: 'I've worked forty-nine years, and most people retire after twenty-five years.' I'm looking forward to not having a job. I can get up when I want to and do what I want to."

* * *

After Driesell came Bob Wade. Most fans generally regard his era as "the disaster." Wade came from Baltimore's Dunbar High School coaching ranks with high marks—but the stretch to college coaching was too much for him. In three seasons Wade's teams won only thirty-six games total and a disappointing seven in the ACC. Still, Wade had some outstanding players, including Adrian Branch, Derrick Lewis, Steve Hood, John Johnson, Keith Gatlin, and Jeff Baxter.

Their talent wasn't enough. Wade resigned under intense pressure during an NCAA investigation that pointed to recruiting and other violations by members of his staff. This is what Gary Williams inherited when he returned to his alma mater.

I first met Williams in 1980, when he coached a good team at American University. He was extremely enthusiastic on the sidelines, pumped up every time his Eagles took the court. From American he went on to coach Boston College and then Ohio State University.

Former Maryland sports information director Jack Zane walked into Cole early one morning just after Williams was hired at Maryland. Zane saw the coach leaning against a rail, looking down on the court. "Are you reminiscing about the old days?" asked Zane. "No," said Williams, "I'm just concentrating on the things we have to do."

Williams elaborated on those days for *TERP* magazine: "It seemed to me the university needed an attitude adjustment. As a coach, I am always looking at attitude, and I felt the university was afraid to say how good it was, afraid to say our programs were among the best in the country . . . I can get stubborn; remember, I am from New Jersey. When you are backed into a corner, you just fight your way out. My experience as a player helped in that situation. I stayed positive about the fact that we could be a great program, and I wasn't afraid to talk about it and to work through it."

During his student days at Maryland (1964–66), Williams served as team captain and starting guard. The future of Maryland basketball might have been radically different had he decided to attend Clemson instead. Both schools recruited

Young student-athlete Gary Williams (14) shows quickness in beating a Clemson Tiger to the hoop.

Williams after watching him score 27 points in a Collingswood High School game.

In fact, Williams had almost packed for Clemson when his high school coach, John Smith, persuaded him that Maryland was the better place, with a better, more upbeat coaching staff. The athletic scholarship that Maryland offered clinched the deal, and Williams went on to become the first member of his family to get a college degree. Coach Smith still keeps in contact with his former player and was on hand to see Williams cut down the championship net in Atlanta in 2002. "Gary as a player is pretty much the same as he is today," says Smith.

At Maryland, Williams lettered four years straight in basketball and baseball. As a basketball player, he was a perfect 8 for 8 from the field in a game against South Carolina in 1966. The swift-breaking offense that you see in today's Maryland teams is not unlike the offense that Vic Bubas's Duke team used against the Terps when Williams was competing on the court.

Even so, Williams often credits Coach Bud Millikan for helping him formulate facets of his approach. Williams's coat and tie at game time are nods to the Millikan style, but the real deal is his focus on defense. In his 2002 autobiography, *Sweet Redemption*, Williams said this of his former coach: "You couldn't play for Bud Millikan unless you were willing to play hard on the defensive end of the court. In practice, we would practice two and a half hours of defense and spend about ten minutes on offense . . . Under Bud you had to take charge and dive on the ball. I had played that way in high school, but I still had to learn all of his techniques. For instance, if your man didn't have the ball, he knew where you should be on the court, and he

Lefty Driesell (with ball) congratulates Gary Williams at the Comcast Center on becoming all-time winningest Maryland coach. Courtesy of William Vaughan

demanded that you play a certain distance from your man. If you didn't play defense his way, you didn't play."

Williams developed a preference for the full-court pressure defense that his Terrapins now play. By his junior year in college, he had decided that coaching was his future. During his fifth year at Maryland, while earning a marketing degree, Williams became assistant coach to Tom Davis for the freshman team. Two years later Williams, as head coach of Woodrow Wilson High School in Camden, New Jersey, launched his team to a 27–0 record and the state championship.

A much bigger championship came in 2002, when the Terps won the NCAA title under Williams's leadership. After that win, the coach reflected on his upbringing in New Jersey, where he was raised by an intensely private father who was generally disinterested in sports. "We weren't one of those families that were really close," Williams told *Sports Illustrated*. "But the game was always a constant in my life. My parents got divorced, but you could always go shoot [a] basketball if things weren't going well. The great thing about basketball is, if you have a ball and a rim, you can go play and you don't need anybody else around."

One of Williams's standout players also employed basketball to get through a difficult childhood. This fact strengthened the bond between Williams and Juan Dixon, sometimes cited as the one player that Williams could never scare. Williams agrees that Dixon is as tough and competitive as any player he's ever coached. Yet this wasn't the perception in College Park when Williams first recruited Dixon. Many folks—including other college scouts—considered the Baltimore native, who had lost both parents to complications from AIDS, to be too skinny and small. Another obstacle was his SAT testing, which he repeated a few times to make the grade.

That Williams believed in Dixon early on is evident. In his autobiography Williams wrote, "Juan loved to play. I saw that immediately. He was always shooting extra after practice, trying to get better, in part by increasing his range. He went from 17 feet to 19 feet to 22 feet. It was a gradual thing. You take thousands of shots and get your legs stronger in the weight room and all of a sudden, it happens . . . every great shooter I've coached takes more shots after practice. They come back at night or stay and

Gary Williams: Vital Basketball Stats

Born: March 4, 1945, in Collingswood, New Jersey

Alma Mater: Maryland, 1968

Colleges Coached: American (1978–82); Boston College (1982–86); Ohio State (1986–89); Maryland (1989–present)

Winningest coach in Maryland basketball history

Has recorded more than 350 Terp victories and more than 500 career wins in twenty-eight seasons

Won the 2002 NCAA National Championship—the first in Maryland's history

Has made seven Sweet Sixteen appearances; went to two consecutive Final Fours

One of only five NCAA Division I coaches to appear in eleven consecutive NCAA Tournaments (1994–2004)

Engineered the greatest comeback in the fifty-two-year history of the ACC Tournament, when the Terps overcame a 21-point first-half deficit against Duke (2004)

With a victory over number one Florida (December 10, 2003), has defeated more top-ranked teams (six) than any other coach in the nation

Atlantic Coast Conference Coach of the Year (2002)

Inducted into the UM Sports Hall of Fame (1999) and the UM Alumni Hall of Fame (2005)

keep shooting. You have to dedicate part of your social life to become a great shooter. Not many guys want to do that."

It is safe to say that all of Williams's players have been dramatically influenced by his philosophy. Duane Simpkins says that what he learned most from Williams "is that you have to bring it in every day. I'm in awe of Gary's passion and excitement for the game, day-in and day-out." Today, Simpkins coaches high school basketball at Sidwell Friends in Washington, D.C. He says that he would be satisfied to bring just half of Williams's enthusiasm to his own players. "If I can do that, then I'll be well on my way," says Simpkins.

"Gary expects 100 percent at all times," adds Steve Blake. "And that's what I try to remember now when I'm playing in the NBA."

Even state politicians recognize Williams's admirable traits. Governor Robert L. Ehrlich Jr. had this to say about the university coach: "Gary Williams is as intense and loyal an individual as I have ever met. Little wonder that these qualities have made him legions of fans and admirers throughout the intensely competitive world of collegiate basketball."

Many profiles on Williams note that he somehow keeps a part of himself off limits to his friends and fans, a part of himself that nobody else knows. I don't buy that. I have worked with Williams professionally for more than seventeen years, and he's been my friend for just as long. He cares about his players. He hates to lose. He loves his daughter and grandchildren. He values and enjoys his friends. He's forceful. He's a strong individual, unafraid of leadership. He doesn't suffer fools. Basketball is his life. Maryland University is his world. Where's the mystery?

In my autobiography, *From Rock to Jock*, I related a story told to me by former George Washington University coach Bob Tallent. Tallent (then coach at GW) and Williams (then coach at American University) were attending a Washington Bullets outing at Crofton Country Club in the late 1970s. As the sun set on the venue, Tallent's two-year-old son, Matthew, accidentally fell into the 12-foot end of the club swimming pool.

Luckily, Williams saw the accident happen. He instinctively and immediately dove in and pulled Matthew to safety. "In my house, Gary Williams is a saint," Tallent says today. "It was no big deal," said Williams when I reminded him of this incident.

Williams and I have spent much time together as coach and announcer (respectively) at games and on our weekly radio and TV shows. Based on personal observations, I would say that in the days since his team won the 2002 NCAA Championship, Williams has mellowed a tad. He certainly was generous in sharing quotes for this book. One of the things he said speaks volumes about his authentic character.

"As time goes by," Williams told me, "you see your players grow up, get older, get married . . . and I observe how they conduct their lives. People look at your win–loss record, but coaches measure their successes a little differently sometimes. I look at how my guys have done. Many have come back to help with the program. It has been great to watch."

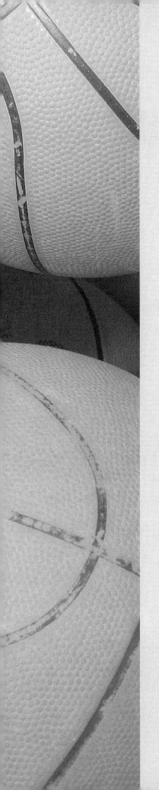

Champions

Coach Gary Williams imposed no curfew on March 31, 2002, the night before Maryland's first NCAA Championship contest. The players were free to absorb the evolving pandemonium as they approached the summit. "We were staying in the hotel along with all the fans and well-wishers," recalls Tahj Holden. "It was good, but it was also hard to focus on the game with everyone—especially all the people who had followed the program for so long—telling us 'good luck.' "

Steve Blake tried to stay as focused as possible. "It was just another game, but at the same time, the biggest game of my life," he remembers. Blake stayed in his room, where family visited to wish him the best of luck. "But," he says, "I was doing a lot of preparing by thinking. Andre Collins dropped by with a bottle of champagne, and we agreed we'd drink it together if we won."

Juan Dixon had honed his natural leadership skills as he and his fellow senior captains, Lonny Baxter and Byron Mouton, led the team to an undefeated 15–0 season at Cole Field House and to their second Final Four. The Terrapins had faced a murderers' row to get to the 2002 NCAA Championship game: Wisconsin, Kentucky, Connecticut, and Kansas. Plus they were playing Indiana, a program with five championships; the Hoosiers had never lost an NCAA final.

* * *

First up in the East Regionals was Siena. The Saints were looking to become the first sixteenth seed to beat a number one, but they had never faced the likes of Dixon and his Terrapin teammates. In leading Maryland to a 85–70 win, Dixon scored 29 points—only 2 points shy of the school record (held by Len Bias and Joe Smith) for most points in an NCAA game. What was impressive about the win was that Maryland had lost in the ACC Tournament semifinals to North Carolina State, 86–82. This loss had snapped a thirteen-game winning streak, but it did not dampen the Terps' enthusiasm.

Dixon was the first to crack a joke in the locker room, and he took it upon himself to keep his fellow players relaxed. The fifth-year senior from Baltimore was always loose before games. When the Terps got to the finals, however, we saw a different side of

Juan Dixon, one of the most beloved Terps of all time, prepares to dunk.
Al Tielemans/Sports Illustrated

him. He became serious and focused. Dixon had already over-come many personal tragedies—the death of his mom and dad to drug complications, and a less-than-ideal childhood. It was fitting that he would now carry the team on his shoulders.

Juan Dixon (#3): Career Stats

6'3" Guard, Baltimore, Maryland
All-American 2001, 2002

Year	Games Played	Assists	Rebounds–Average	Points–Average
1998–99	34	47	88–2.6	250–7.4
1999–2000	35	127	192–5.5	630–18.0
2000–01	36	93	153–4.3	654–18.2
2001–02	36	104	166–4.6	735–20.4
Career	141	371	599–4.2	2,269–16.1

Dixon is Maryland's all-time scoring champ (2,269 points) and the winningest Terp ever (110 victories). He is the only other Terrapin besides John Lucas to be named first-team All-ACC in three straight seasons. Dixon ended his college career as the only player in NCAA history to achieve 2,000 points, 300 steals, and 200 three-pointers, and he never fouled out in 141 career games. He scored in double digits in fifty-four straight games, the second longest streak in Terp history. The Washington Wizards selected him in the 2002 NBA draft.

Two days after ending Siena's season, the Terps advanced to the Sweet Sixteen for the sixth time in nine years. There they calmly battered the Badgers of Wisconsin, 87–57. How dominant was Maryland's performance? The team handed Wisconsin its worst defeat in nineteen NCAA Tournament games.

Once again, Dixon had the fans in the MCI Center on their feet, scoring 29 points for the second consecutive game and breaking two Maryland team records in the process. Dixon retired Len Bias's records for most career points and for career points in the tournament (Dixon raised his totals to 2,172 and 197, respectively).

The Terps were two games away from the Final Four. Next came a matchup against Kentucky in Syracuse. However, a distraction courtesy of the *Washington Post* added to the drama. A front-page story focused on the University of Maryland's alleged low graduation rates for players. Without going into the technical details of the article, let's just say that Gary Williams was not at all pleased with the story and especially not with the timing. Fortunately, Williams didn't have much time to simmer because he had a game to play that evening.

Keith Bogans and Tayshaun Prince both contributed points for the Wildcats early, with Kentucky jumping out to an 8–2 lead. Maryland fought and scratched back to lead at the break, 39–33, after a Chris Wilcox slam dunk with 6 seconds to go.

Prince dialed long-distance with a trey to tie the game at 45 with 16:11 to play. Later, Marquis Estill canned a pair of free throws, and the Cats and Terps were tied at 53. With a little over ten minutes to play, it was anybody's ball game. But Maryland quietly pulled away to earn a bout against Connecticut.

The Terps thought they knew all about UConn. But the Huskies team in Syracuse was much improved over the one Maryland had faced and beaten on December 3, 2001, in the BB&T Classic Basketball Tournament final. Caron Butler had been lighting up every opponent and having his way with every team the Huskies had faced in the tournament. Maryland would be no exception. Hitting on a variety of shots, Butler torched the Terps for 32 points.

Mouton did his best to contain Butler, but no one could stop the Husky that night. Regardless, from the fourteen-minute mark down to the final 36 seconds, neither team led by more than 3 points. Williams called a time-out to set up a play. The strategy was to get the ball into Dixon's hand coming off a screen.

Blake stepped forward. "Hey, Coach," he said. "I can handle things. I'll take the shot." It was quite a brash statement for Blake, who had scored only 4 points against Kentucky and 3 against Wisconsin and had made only 2 free throws in 39 minutes and 25 seconds against the Huskies. But there was no doubt in Blake's mind that he could make the shot. That's the mark of a good, hard-nosed player. He nailed a three-pointer with 25 seconds to go to put the Terps up by 4. They would win it by 8.

With twenty-four lead changes and twenty-one ties, the UConn game proved to be the most exciting contest of the tournament. Nipping the Huskies was the biggest hurdle. Now the Terps were in the Final Four. They had won thirty games for the first time in school history.

Maryland's trip to the Final Four was a solid team effort—a program rarely wins thirty games in a season without having some great talent and cooperation. However, it does take a few

Lonny Baxter, co-captain of
the 2002 NCAA champions,
drives the lane.
UM Athletic Department

Lonny Baxter (#35): Career Stats

6'8" Forward, Silver Spring, Maryland
All-American 2002

Year	Games Played	Assists	Rebounds–Average	Points–Average
1998–99	32	18	116–3.6	217–6.8
1999–2000	35	31	308–8.8	547–15.6
2000–01	36	19	286–7.9	561–15.6
2001–02	35	28	288–8.2	533–15.2
Career	138	96	998–7.2	1,858–13.5

Baxter, a powerful bruiser with excellent hands and touch around the basket, became just the tenth player in NCAA history to earn NCAA Regional honors in consecutive seasons. He guided Maryland to two Final Four appearances and shares the school record for most career starts (sixteen) in the NCAA Tournament.

Baxter finished his Terp career as Maryland's second leading rebounder and its sixth leading scorer of all time. He was also a three-time All-ACC player, earning first-team honors in 2000 and second-team accolades as a junior and senior. Baxter was selected by the Chicago Bulls in the 2002 NBA draft.

dominating performances every now and then. Baxter was forceful against the Huskies, scoring 29 points and grabbing 9 rebounds; he also showed a deft touch at the line, converting 15 of his 18 free throw attempts. As a team, the Terps missed only four free throws all night long.

After the victory over UConn, the next stop was Atlanta, Georgia, where the Terps faced the Kansas Jayhawks in the Final Four. Kansas led the nation in scoring. Undefeated in the Big 12 Conference during the regular season, the Jayhawks also had won thirty-three of their thirty-six games, and like the Terrapins, they preferred to keep the game up-tempo. Kansas had plenty of outstanding players, including Drew Gooden, Kirk Hinrich, and Nick Collison, so Maryland had reason to be concerned. Both teams were almost identical in playing style. Both were legitimate contenders for the championship.

Kansas jumped out to an 11-point lead in the first four minutes. This jackrabbit start by the Jayhawks had Maryland supporters very uncomfortable, perhaps thinking back to the Final Four loss in 2001. Baxter got into foul trouble early, playing only three minutes in the first half.

With the score at 13–3, Coach Williams called a time-out. He was ready to berate the team, but Dixon started grabbing guys, telling them how hard they had to play. "Of course," says Williams, "Juan, being Juan, went out and next hit two three-pointers to bring it to 13–9. Juan talked a lot, but he backed up everything he said. In that game we probably played our best stretch of basketball that year. We outscored a very good Kansas team 35–7 in the next twenty-minute period over the course of the first and second half. Then Kansas made a run at us, and Juan hit a big shot to stop the run and got us to the championship game."

Many things had fallen into place for the Terps in 2002, including a lack of serious injuries. A sense of team cohesiveness was there. The desire and necessary skill were there. Still, nobody thought it would be easy to win the whole thing. "That 2002 crew was strong, just tremendous, with Juan Dixon, Steve Blake, Chris Wilcox, and Lonny Baxter," says Williams. "The other thing about that team that some may have forgot is that we had the biggest team in the country that year. Coming off the bench we had Tahj Holden at 6'11" and 260 pounds; Ryan Randle was 6'9" and 250 pounds. And we had another weapon, Drew Nicholas, and he played quite a bit that year. He became one of the best shooters to ever play at Maryland and was important to the team. In fact, he was on the floor at the end of the championship game."

* * *

The 2001–02 Terps' resolve to return to the Final Four was palpable in October, at the very first practice of the season. Then-freshman Mike Grinnon remembers getting kicked in the face by Chris Wilcox as Chris dunked the ball during a pickup game. "Think about it," asserts Grinnon. "I'm 6'6", and I get kicked in the face. It was a reality shock that made me realize the level of playing and intimidation this team was capable of."

It certainly showed on the hardwoods in Atlanta. *Baltimore Sun* reporter Paul McMullen provides a good summation of the championship game in his fine book *Maryland Basketball*: "Dixon personally outscored Indiana in the first nine minutes as the Terps took a 19–8 lead, but then Hoosier defensive stopper

Dane Fife kept the ball out of his hands and a football-sized crowd of 53,406 got behind the underdog. Tom Coverdale hit some difficult three-pointers, and Indiana took its first lead at 44–42 on a low-post move by Jared Jeffries, but the Terp deficit would last all of seven seconds. Fife gambled and helped out on a trap of Blake, whose NCAA highlights had been restricted to the three against Connecticut. The junior split the double team, took the ball right to the basket, and kicked a laser back to Dixon on the left wing. A few minutes earlier, Dixon had pointed to his brother Phil in the stands and said 'It's all right, it's all right,' and he made it right with his first points in 20 minutes, sinking a three-pointer that put Maryland back on top to stay."

Looking back today, Holden confirms the team's dedication to take it all. "Anything less than a NCAA Championship wouldn't have been good enough for the team," says Holden, "especially after we lost in the Final Four the previous season. I said from the beginning that we were going to win it, so I shed no tears when the buzzer sounded. I felt joy and relief."

Holden cites Nick Collison of Kansas and Caron Butler of UConn as his toughest opponents during the Terrapins' run to the title game: "Collison was one of the most fundamentally sound players I had to guard. He could run the court, rebound, defend, and had a nice little jump shot. Besides him, there was Caron. I remember [him] getting into early foul trouble when we played UConn, and he came back in the second half with 26 points. We put pretty much everybody against him—Juan Dixon, Byron Mouton, and I ended up guarding him."

Holden says that nerves played a role at the beginning of the championship game. "It was a defensive struggle. Indiana had an underrated defensive team with Jared Jeffries, a very versatile guard. Some of the team tired because Coach had to change all of our guards around."

But the tension began much sooner. Referee Tony Green recalls one moment in particular: "Juan was warming up before the game," he says. "I could see it in his eyes. He looked at me with a glassy stare, sweat already running down his face, and Juan says, 'It's on tonight.' "

In the pregame moments, Green told both teams to go out and put the ball in the basket. "That really didn't happen," the ref says now, referring to the relatively low final score of 64–52. "Still, there were some athletic moments to be proud of. I really liked how Juan Dixon and Steve Blake teamed up to make things happen on the floor. But the one guy I thought was unbelievable overall for Maryland during that game and the entire season was Chris Wilcox."

Wilcox had 10 points (shooting 4 for 8 from the field), 7 rebounds, no assists, and 3 fouls in his twenty-four minutes against Indiana. When the final buzzer blew, Green says, Wilcox told supporters, "I'm outta here" —evidently indicating his desire to enter the NBA.

Coach Williams offers a final reflection: "It was a great defensive effort by both teams. You don't usually win a championship game by 12 points. Neither team shot the ball very well, but once again we got a little bit of a lead. Indiana made a run, but Juan made a shot on the baseline, and that stopped Indiana. We had a very good team, and four guys—Dixon, Blake, Wilcox, and Baxter—were eventually drafted into the NBA."

Steve Blake (left) picks a Wolfpack player's pocket. Al Tielemans/Sports Illustrated

Steve Blake (#25): Career Stats

6'3" Guard, Miami, Florida
All-American 2002

Year	Games Played	Assists	Rebounds– Average	Points– Average
1999–2000	35	217	106–3.0	244–7.0
2000–01	36	248	108–3.0	248–6.9
2001–02	36	286	137–3.8	287–8.0
2002–03	31	221	114–3.7	360–11.6
Career	138	972	465–3.4	1,139–8.3

After the NCAA Championship, Blake opted out of the NBA draft and returned to Maryland, finishing his Terp days as the school's all-time leader in assists, games started, and minutes played. He led the ACC in assists as a sophomore, junior, and senior, and he is the only player in ACC history with 1,000 points, 800 assists, and 400 rebounds. Blake played every game of his four-year career, which included three Sweet Sixteen appearances, two trips to the Final Four, a national title, and fifteen NCAA Tournament games. His 4,312 minutes played are more than any other Maryland Terrapin.

Monday, April 1, 2002, was a beautiful, warm, and sunny day in Atlanta. It was no April Fool's joke: Maryland made its first appearance in a national championship game with a school record of thirty-one victories to face an Indiana team that had surprised the experts by beating Oklahoma.

As I sat on press row, I couldn't help but think I was watching history. And as the final seconds ticked off in the Terps' 64–52 victory over the Hoosiers, I found it difficult to deal with the emotions of broadcasting a championship game. I knew that the impact of winning would be felt forever in the hearts of Terp fans. Like Coach Williams—and so many former Maryland coaches, players, and fans—I had wondered what it might feel like to be NCAA champions.

My color analyst partner, Chris Knoche, and I certainly found out. It's a feeling I want to have again and again.

The homecoming was even sweeter. "Our reception coming off the plane was amazing," says Blake. "I didn't expect it. We traveled down I–95 from the airport with a helicopter escort overhead, and Cole Field House was packed with fans when we got there. It was awesome."

Home Court Advantages

One of many emotional highlights for Maryland fans came on March 3, 2002, when the second-ranked Terps upset number one–ranked Virginia in the final game held at Cole Field House. It was the seventh time in history that a number one team had lost to Maryland in Cole—home of more upsets of top-ranked teams than any other facility in the country.

On that same day Lonny Baxter, Juan Dixon, Byron Mouton, and Earl Badu were honored as part of the Senior Day celebration. The four Terps totaled 56 points against the Cavaliers.

The packed-in crowd cheered, cried, and cheered some more. It was very moving. Coach Gary Williams worried that his players might "get caught up in emotions" because every great living Maryland basketball player—more than fifty in all—returned to see the last men's basketball game played in Cole. Among the notables were early Terrapins who contributed to the history of Maryland sports, including members of the 1955–56 and 1957–58 teams. Also returning were All-Americans Keith Booth, Len Elmore, Tom McMillen, Walt Williams, Ernie Graham, and Larry Gibson. Gibson was the only Terp to be voted team MVP for three consecutive seasons.

"You could not get a ticket, except for thousands of bucks on eBay," says Williams. "Many people had grown up and grown old going to Cole Field House. And Virginia was an impressive team."

The Cavaliers never threatened the Terps. Maryland held a 7-point lead at halftime but really put away the game in the opening minutes of the second half, when Baxter scored 6 points and Dixon 5. An 18–6 run widened the lead to 19 points. Freshman Andre Collins is now in the Terp trivia books as having scored the final field goal at Cole.

With the win the Terps finished 16–0 at home, securing the ACC regular season title. "We really played well," says Williams. "To close Cole down in that manner is something I will always remember."

For many who have followed the program through good and bad times, the highlight of the evening came when several generations of Maryland players passed the ball from one to another. It was fitting that the ball went from the hands of Bud Millikan to Williams, his former player. For Coach Millikan it was much more than a nostalgic evening. He had invested his heart and his life's work in Cole. He still remembers when the administration told him that they had plans to build a new arena for the College of Physical Education. It was 1951, and Millikan had just been hired at Maryland.

"We had been playing in Ritchie, and that was just like one of your little old high school gyms," he says. Ritchie Coliseum had opened in 1931, replacing a facility simply known as "the Gymnasium." The newer arena—named after Albert Cabell Ritchie, then the Maryland governor and a 1932 candidate for the Democratic nomination for president—held 1,500 people. It was home to Maryland basketball and the more popular boxing matches for twenty-four years.

"The crowds were small at first but started picking up when we joined the ACC in 1953," Millikan remembers. "We had a full house most nights at Ritchie. I told [football coach] Jim Tatum that the only thing he ever did that really ticked me off was when he put in the papers, 'Don't bother to try and get tickets because the games are all sold out.' " Millikan went to Tatum's office and told him that this was the wrong approach. "I thought we should be getting students standing in line from Baltimore to D.C., trying to get into the damn games. Please don't tell people the games are sold out."

On December 2, 1955, Cole Field House opened its doors; 9,000 fans were on hand to witness the Terps defeat the Virginia Cavaliers, 67–55. Jack Heise was there for the opening game, the

At Ritchie Coliseum, basketball
followed the boxing matches.

last game, and about 600 in between. "It was a very different atmosphere that first game," says Heise. "It was like the ball team was on a stage. The courtside seats would come later with Lefty. This was a sharp contrast to what it was like in Ritchie, where the team was almost in the seats with the students. There were about ten of us who had season tickets at Ritchie, and we got to choose our new seats at Cole."

Bob Kessler scored the first points in the new arena on a pair of free throws. He wound up with 23 points in that game in 1955. Soon Millikan was seeing 13,000 fans on hand. The players really responded, thanks to the coach's classy style and focus on defense. In 1957–58 the Terps—with such standouts as Gerry Bechtle, Tom Young, and the late Nick Davis—went 22–7; they made it to the regionals of the NCAA Tournament.

When it debuted, Cole was the largest basketball arena in the East after Madison Square Garden. Officially, it was the William P. Cole Jr. Student Activities Building, named after Judge William P. Cole Jr., who was chairman of the university's board of regents from 1944 to 1956. Many folks at the time, including the editors of the *Diamondback* student newspaper, questioned whether Cole was worth its hefty price tag of $3.3 million. Boy, were they wrong.

In 1965 the Terps won eighteen games and went 10–4 in the ACC. Joe Harrington was a member of that Millikan team, as was Gary Williams. Harrington says that the first memory that comes to mind is "playing Penn State. Neil Brayton made a shot at the buzzer to win. It was hot in Cole, and loud."

No longtime Terrapin fan will ever forget the slowdown game on January 9, 1971, when the Terps faced South Carolina

The venerable Cole Field House. Painting courtesy of the artist, Mary Holliday

at Cole. Neither will former player Jim O'Brien. He recalls: "Carolina came into Cole ranked number one. It was a big event in the papers and a lot of excitement when Carolina came in because there had been a big fight at South Carolina the first time Maryland played them that season. When they came back up to Maryland, Coach Driesell was afraid for the team's safety, and he wasn't sure if they should even play us. Cole was packed. We stole the ball three straight inbounds plays."

This was in the era before the shot clock. Each team had taken only two shots in the first half, with Maryland leading 4–3 at halftime. It would be the fewest points that Maryland scored that year and the fewest they gave up.

An O'Brien layup tied the game with 5 seconds to go in regulation. O'Brien then hit an 11-foot jumper with 4 seconds remaining, and the Terps won the contest, 31–30. Teammate Jap Trimble from Philadelphia remembers: "It was phenomenal to be there. I was a freshman playing when Jimmy O hit the basket that won the game. Cole went crazy. I couldn't talk for three days. It was phenomenal to be there."

Cole also hosted a variety of special events when the Terps weren't playing. In 1962 the arena held its first East Regionals. NYU beat St. John's in the final, 94–85. Cole hosted its first Final Four in 1966, with Kentucky, Texas Western, Utah, and Duke taking the floor. Most college basketball fans know the significance of that title game: Texas Western's all–African-American starting lineup defeated an all-white Kentucky team coached by Adolph Rupp.

In the early 1970s the Capital Bullets—now the Washington Wizards—played their home games at Cole as they made their move from Baltimore to D.C. And in 1972 the first sporting event between the People's Republic of China and the United States was held in Cole. In an attempt to open relations with China, President Richard Nixon had offered plans to end the twenty-year embargo on trade with that nation. The Chinese table tennis

UM Athletic Hall of Fame: Men's Basketball Inductees

Inductee/Class	Year	Inductee/Class	Year
Louis W. Berger/1932	1982	Thomas A. Mont/1947	1987
Joseph C. Burger/1925	1982	John D. Gilmore Jr./1943	1988
John W. Guckeyson/1936	1982	Herman A. "Bud" Millikan	1988
Charles E. Keller/1937	1982	Victor G. Willis/1937	1988
Frederick C. Linkous/1928	1982	Edward Ronkin/1932	1989
Julius J. Radice/1930	1982	Charles A. May/1931	1990
William C. Supplee/1926	1982	Milton M. Mulitz/1940	1990
George V. Chalmers/1932	1983	Myron B. Stevens/1927	1990
William W. Evans/1930	1983	Gene Shue/1954	1991
Norwood S. Sothoron/1935	1983	Tom McMillen/1974	1995
Albert B. Heagy/1930	1984	John Lucas/1974	1996
Pershing L. Mondorff/1941	1984	Len Elmore/1974	1997
Francis A Buscher/1934	1986	Gary Williams/1968	1999
James H. Kehoe, Jr./1940	1986	Buck Williams/1981	2001
John W. Zane/1960	1986	Tom Young/1958	2003
George W. Knepley/1939	1987	Walt Williams/1992	2005

team responded by visiting the United States. This "ping-pong diplomacy," as it came to be known, was a historic event.

Elvis Presley, Janis Joplin, Bob Dylan, and James Taylor are a few of the notable musicians who played Cole. Still, nobody rocked the house like the Terps. In forty-seven seasons, 638 basketball games were played at Cole.

The House That Gary Built

The Comcast Center—also known as "The House That Gary Built" or simply "Garyland"—opened its doors in October 2002. Women's head coach Brenda Frese, then in her first year, introduced her Maryland squad at Midnight Madness. Williams, then starting his fourteenth season at Maryland, followed with the men's team, as the Terps began their eightieth consecutive basketball season at UM.

The $125 million Comcast Center, with a capacity of 17,950, hosted the first official men's game in 2005, a 64–49 win over Miami University of Ohio. Comcast also features a 1,500-seat gymnasium for volleyball, gymnastics, and wrestling; an academic support center; a 400-seat banquet hall; and the offices of the athletics department. On the east side of the entrance is the Terrapin Walk of Fame and History. It features sharp images from the past of Maryland athletics, along with the 2002 men's NCAA trophy and the 2006 women's NCAA trophy.

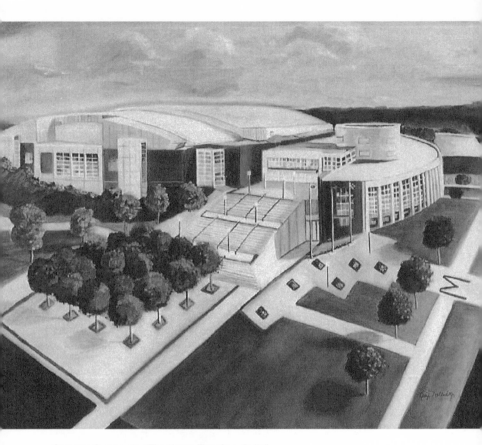

Comcast Center, aka "The House That Gary Built."
Painting courtesy of the artist, Mary Holliday

The student section comprises 4,000 seats arranged in the first ten rows on all sides of the arena. Williams insisted on this. Then there are high-pitched seats behind the opposing team's second-half basket. Known as "The Wall," this area has 2,600 Terrapin fan seats to help discourage the accuracy of opponents' free throws.

In just three short years at Comcast, Maryland's home attendance soared, averaging more than 17,200 spectators per game. The arena is a dynamic facility for fans and an absolutely spectacular showcase for student athletes—both Williams's men and Frese's women—to display their athletic prowess and basketball skills.

Speaking of Frese, look what she has accomplished with the women's basketball program in just four short years. In 2006 she led her squad to Maryland's fourth Final Four—and the first Women's NCAA National Championship in school history. The Lady Terps came back from a 13-point deficit, tying the game on a clutch three-point shot by freshman Kristi Toliver (from Harrisonburg, Virginia) with 6.1 seconds left. Maryland went on to win in overtime against the favored Blue Devils, 78–75.

Score One for the Women

The Comcast Center is now home to two national champions. On April 4, 2006, the Lady Terps earned their first NCAA title by beating Duke 78–75. Inside the home arena in College Park, a piece of the Boston championship court hangs next to a piece of hardwood from Atlanta, where the Terrapin men won their national title in 2002. The women's championship trophy shines in the display case at the entrance to the arena.

Coach Frese won thirty-four games in 2005–06, more than any men or women's basketball team at Maryland ever. "You hope that we're building a dynasty here," she said after the NCAA win in Boston. "But each and every season defines its own, the players define it with their character and really how they come together, and so you really have to take each team as its own."

Summing up the entire Maryland sports program, athletics director Debbie Yow says, "We have the finest student-athletes, coaches, support staff, and administrative team in America. It is because of their courage, hard work, and cooperative spirit that we now have a strong, viable athletic program."

For Coach Williams, his team, and every Terp supporter, the goals of the basketball program remain the same: to win another ACC Tournament and another national championship.

Lofty goals? Absolutely. Achievable? You can bet on it.

Fear the Terps.

About the Author

Johnny Holliday (right) with Albert King.

Hall of Fame broadcaster Johnny Holliday has been the voice of Maryland Terrapins men's basketball and football since 1979 on statewide radio networks and on the coaches' TV shows. For twenty-six years, his daily sports report has been heard on the ABC Radio Networks, as has his live coverage from the Olympic Games. Holliday first gained national recognition in 1959 as a rock 'n' roll disc jockey. He was named America's number one Top 40 disc jockey in 1965, and his work is included in the Rock and Roll Hall of Fame.

From his public address duties with the Cleveland Browns, Oakland Raiders, and Golden State Warriors to his work in Washington radio and television for the Bullets, Senators, Redskins, and Orioles, Holliday has made a complicated business look easy. In 2002 Holliday published his autobiography, *From Rock to Jock*, with coauthor Stephen Moore.

Stephen Moore, who assisted in the writing of this book, is a University of Maryland grad and currently is director of Advanced Research Computing (ARC) with the Office of Information Services at Georgetown University. A member of the Author's Guild and a veteran rock musician with thirty years' experience on the Washington, D.C., music scene, Moore has written 100-plus articles for publications that include the *Washingtonian, Stagebill,* the *Times-Journal,* and *Rolling Stone.* With Donn B. Murphy, he coauthored *Helen Hayes: A Biography,* which detailed the exceptionally long career of the "First Lady of American Theatre." Moore lives in Bethesda, Maryland.

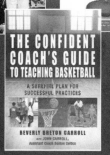